God Called Love

God Called Love

Michael J. Chanley

Published in the United States by ChurchLit Publishing.
All rights reserved.
Author: Michael J. Chanley

Cover Design: Michael J. Chanley & Cori Horvath
Editors: Laura Meyer & Matt Stottmann
Author photo: Kevin Mosier

Hardcover ISBN: 979-8-9892277-0-9
Paperback ISBN: 979-8-9892277-9-2
Ebook/Digital ISBN: 979-8-9892277-3-0

.

Subjects: Jesus Christ, New Testament, Bible Study, Christianity, Faith, Hope, Love, Agape, Christian Living, Spiritual Formation, John, Peter, Gospel of John, Gospel, Religion, Christian Church

Bulk sales discounts may be available. To inquire, please contact sales@churchlit.com.

For speaking engagements, email: office@michaeljchanley.com.

Hope & Honeybess - Lessons of Faith From a Local Beekeeper

Escape: The Traps of Christianity

Escape: The Traps of Christianity Journal

Chasing WHALES: A Spiritual Dive with Jonah

Collaborate: Family + Church

The Art of Parenting: Nurturing Happy, Confident, and Resilient Children

Get the companion study to *God Called Love*.

Experiencing God Called Love: 5 Week Journal on God's Love & Spiritual Practices Guidebook, a resource designed with tools to enhance your ability to study and learn from God's Word, including:

- 35 Day Bible Study highlighting God's perfect, (agape) love

- 5 Week Prayer and Fasting journal with guided pages.

- Spiritual Practices Guidebook with a section on how to pray.

- New Testament reading plan

- Excerpts from "God Called Love"

For Atticus, and all who follow.
May you find the goodness of God and His perfect love.

CONTENTS

U nconditional love invites us into a relationship. It demands our attention.

In pursuit of faith, the follower of Christ must soon reconcile the exceptional love of God. It is a supernatural love able to deny the self, even at great cost to all we hold dear. However, such a heady definition of love invites us into a deeper conversation. It beckons us to consider the heartfelt origins of such a love.

What does unconditional love mean to me?

Where does it come from?
How do I experience this greatest of all loves?

In my experience, love is difficult to grasp and much more difficult to live out. Our world often corrupts our concept of love.

We make love self-centered.

We make it about us.

We fail to understand it; therefore, we fail to live out the love shown to and commanded of us as ambassadors of Christ. This conflict within our souls, where we claim to worship a God of love but scream at our neighbors, invites us to a deeper study.

Recently, love has been heavy on my heart.

As a seminary student, I studied the ancient writings about love and witnessed, through countless writings, the devotion others have felt to God's perfect, all-inviting love. Yet, the heaviness I felt was in seeing how people who proclaim to be Christians treat one another with absolute hate and disdain.

It was unsettling.

I embarked on a quest. A quest to understand love. In my boldness, I decided to make the exploration of God's love a year-long search. I read books about love, studied the subject, and delved into the Bible. I began a Facebook group to invite others to learn with me in the process.

Spoiler alert, a year stretched to two, and I have no reason now to doubt it will take many more years, but more on that later.

A better question, here at the beginning, may be to ask: "Why was I disillusioned with the definition of love?"

Great question. I'm glad you asked.

An atheist in a podcast I was listening to questioned the host, "How could you believe God to be all-loving yet permitting so much suffering?" It's a question worth wrestling with, and it is a challenge that creates in many people a tremendous amount of anxiety.

How does the God of grace, love, and mercy also, seemingly, turn a blind eye to our hardships? We must grapple with this profound question.

What do we, as followers of Christ, say to the atheists?

To the unbelieving?

To the haters?

The doubters?

The critics?

What do we say of ourselves when we fail to live up to the standard of self-sacrificing and perfect love raised upon the cross of Christ?

So, I began a quest and, like many epics, my steps brought me back to my own origin. I returned to where I started my faith journey, the Book of John.

John's Account

John has a lot to say about God's love.

He has answers for the critics.

He has answers for the followers.

He has answers for all.

John's writings often express the love of God for all people.

Who is John?

Why should we care about what he has to say about God, about Jesus?

What can he teach us about God's special sacrificial love?

Understanding the Book of John became essential to my journey of exploring and rediscovering God's love. Therefore, a good place to begin is attempting to understand who wrote the good news attributed to this man named John.

There are at least five theories explaining who wrote the Book of John.

The "Ideal" Disciple - Some believe John is a typecast character meant to represent an ideal disciple, "the one Jesus loved." He's simply the premium model of a loved disciple. That doesn't hold up to scrutiny when we read the other gospel accounts. To be thorough, it is worth mentioning. However, there are many stronger arguments for the author's identity.

The Resurrected Lazarus - Others have argued that the author may be Lazarus, the man raised from the dead by Jesus. They argue that the Book of John is his gospel. However, that perspective doesn't hold up to scrutiny either.

John Mark - Another perspective suggests John Mark, the disciple, was the author. Like these previous theories, upon closer scrutiny (outside the scope of this book), it doesn't fit the bill. Most scholarly work debunks this idea.

John the Baptist - Some early writers suggest the writer could be the last prophet of the Old Testament, John the Baptist. However, John is beheaded before the completion of the events recorded in the Gospel of John. This theory seems to be based primarily on the association of having the same given name, "John." It is an easy attribution to make. Honestly, there are just too many Johns.

John, son of Zebedee - This is most likely the right John. He is the traditionally held author. His identity as the author has been the predominant theory handed down over the centuries. He is called early in Jesus' ministry, and his death occurs after the events recorded in the Book of John. Furthermore, John, son of Zebedee, as one of the original twelve disciples, would have been either present for or in close proximity to the events written about in John's Gospel.

In one commentary I consulted, the *Evangelical Commentary*, Burge writes that:

> "The best solution is the traditional one: John the son of Zebedee (Mark 3:17; Acts 1:13). This man was one of the Twelve and along with James and Peter formed an inner circle around Jesus. This is the origin of his eyewitness testimony and penetrating insight. In the Synoptics John appears with Peter more than with any other and in Acts they are companions in Jerusalem (Acts 3–4) as well as in Samaria

(Acts 8:14). This dovetails with the Peter/John connection in the fourth Gospel." [1]

The Books bearing John's moniker are most likely written down by John himself or those who sat at his feet and listened to him preaching. The Gospel of John, dated by scholars to have been written around 90 AD, is likely composed before the end of John's life and shortly after the death of Jesus.

John, son of Zebedee, who Jesus called while he fished alongside his family, chooses to follow Jesus. The Book of Mark records this moment for us:

> [19] When he [Jesus] had gone a little farther, he saw James son of Zebedee and his brother John in a boat, preparing their nets. [20] Without delay he called them, and they left their father Zebedee in the boat with the hired men and followed him. [2]

John follows Jesus and becomes one of the original twelve disciples and, most likely, the one who authored the fourth gospel account of Jesus' teachings and life, the book that bears the name John.

Why does considering the authorship matter at all? Well, if we are going to explore a book that highlights and explains the complete love of God as a primary source, we need to understand the perspective of the person God used to put pen to paper. Understanding the authorship helps us know the authority and authenticity of the written material. Otherwise, we can be left asking, but did that really happen?

Well, it did happen, and yes, it certainly does matter.

John was one of the original twelve disciples.

He is an eyewitness to Jesus' ministry and life.

His account and retelling of Jesus' ministry have the weight and authority necessary to ground our faith.

Understanding the Book of John as an eyewitness account impacts how we read and understand it. Importantly, it helps us apply it to our original question: What is unconditional love?

A Unique Perspective

John's gospel is tremendously important because John's story of Jesus is unique in many ways.

Of the four eyewitness accounts written about Jesus' teachings, Matthew, Mark, Luke, and John, the Gospel of John stands out.

Even from the beginning verses of John's account, a unique and distinct tone is evident. While the other three writers begin with genealogies, or the story of John the Baptist, the Book of John takes us back to the origin of all things. John's gospel begins with the Genesis moment. The *Bible Knowledge Commentary* points out that...

> "John begins with a theological prologue. It is almost as if John had said, "I want you to consider Jesus in His teaching and deeds. But you will not understand the good news of Jesus in its fullest sense unless you view Him from this point of view. Jesus is God manifest in the flesh, and His words and deeds are those of the God-Man."[3]

John's gospel begins with a profound statement of authority. He proclaims the story of the God of all creation. The story of absolute and unconditional love, passed down to us from a firsthand witness of Christ's life, teachings, suffering, resurrection, and love.

John's gospel is also distinct in its purpose, his audience is broader when compared to that of the other gospel writers. We observe this when considering the intended audience of each gospel letter.

Matthew - Matthew, the first book of the New Testament, is written to the religious Jewish leaders who understood the Old Testament writings and prophecies. He leverages many of the prophecies foretelling the Messiah in his account of Jesus' story.

Mark - Mark, the shortest and most action-packed of the gospels, seems to have written his account for the busy Roman world. His more condensed account brings into focus a sense of forward motion and excitement. It challenges the reader to act.

Luke - Luke, the only author in the Bible who is non-Jewish, writes to the Greeks, or Greek-like Romans. The culture he addresses loves the study of knowledge. In many cases, the readers of Luke's account of Jesus' life are obsessed with wealth and power. Luke appears to take special care in portraying Jesus as an underdog chosen by God to overturn the world's broken ways.

John - John seems to cater to his audience, reaching both the secular and faith-based worlds. He writes a message intended to reach all of humanity. He does so by explaining the deity of Jesus Christ and the love of God in the most absolute and concrete of terms, again, beginning with the laying of the foundations of the entire universe.

In his own words, John writes about his purpose for writing the story of Jesus' life. It is written for us in John 20:30-31.

> [30] Jesus performed many other signs in the presence of his disciples, which are not recorded in this book. [31] But these are written that you may believe that Jesus is the Messiah, the Son of God, and that by believing you may have life in his name. [4]

John explains that he writes distinctly so that you and I may believe, and that by believing, we may have life given to us in the name of Jesus Christ.

Furthermore, John's unique perspective does not come about on its own. He is a disciple of Jesus. We know John is writing with authority from Jesus Himself. John is acting in response to a direct command from Jesus, with the help of the Holy Spirit.

Consider John 15:26-27, where John records Jesus' words.

> [26] "When the Advocate [Holy Spirit] comes, whom I will send to you from the Father—the Spirit of truth who goes out from the Father—he will testify about me. [27] And you also must testify, for you have been with me from the beginning. [5]

Each of the four gospel narratives seeks to provide a testimony of what they witnessed as disciples of Christ. Importantly, we see they are doing so based upon the directions of Christ Himself.

John, in his unique perspective, does not simply begin with an accounting of what he experienced but with the intent of connecting Jesus' profound love with the origins of all things. John goes all the way back to the beginning of time. As he does, he helps his readers to see that there is authority connected to God's love for all the world.

It is a God called love who defines His unconditional love for all people, everywhere, and across all of time.

God Called Love

In his later writings, John continues to clarify God's love by equating God with love. In 1 John 4, he urges his readers to "love one another, for love comes from God" and then goes on to proclaim: "God is love." [6]

This comes from 1 John 4:8-12:

> [8] Whoever does not love does not know God, because God is love. [9] This is how God showed his love among us: He sent his one and only Son into the world that we might live through him. [10] This is love: not

that we loved God, but that he loved us and sent his Son as an atoning sacrifice for our sins. ¹¹ Dear friends, since God so loved us, we also ought to love one another. ¹² No one has ever seen God; but if we love one another, God lives in us and his love is made complete in us. [7]

God is love.

He has demonstrated that love to us.

He is the Creator of love.

Therefore, John writes, since God loves us, we ought to be transformed into creatures of love, capable of love for one another. When we live in such a manner, His "love is made complete in us." [8]

The perfect gift of love is available to all through Jesus Christ. John continues in 1 John 4 by exclaiming this to all who will hear:

> ¹⁵ If anyone acknowledges that Jesus is the Son of God, God lives in them and they in God. ¹⁶ And so we know and rely on the love God has for us.
>
> God is love. Whoever lives in love lives in God, and God in them. ¹⁷ This is how love is made complete among us so that we will have confidence on the day of judgment: In this world we are like Jesus. ¹⁸ There is no fear in love. But perfect love drives out fear, because fear has to do with punishment. The one who fears is not made perfect in love.
>
> ¹⁹ We love because he first loved us. ²⁰ Whoever claims to love God yet hates a brother or sister is a liar. For whoever does not love their brother and sister, whom they have seen, cannot love God, whom they have not seen. ²¹ And he has given us this command: Anyone who loves God must also love their brother and sister. [9]

As we begin to explore the love of God together, keep in mind these two key phrases: "God is love" and "there is no fear in love." [10] Perfect love is able to free us from anxiety and worry because it brings forth grace, truth, and mercy.

In God, love abounds. When we are walking with God, love should flow freely from us as well.

This is not to say there are no consequences for actions, nor is it an attempt to reject the judgment of God, because God is righteous in His love; He is also the judge. The Bible speaks clearly on these matters. This project, however, is simply an invitation to meditate on the love of God, as I have through the studies leading to this book.

God is called love by the Apostle John.

May we each follow Jesus in such a manner that we too begin to know Him as the God called love.

1

Word of God

John 1:1-18 & 1 Peter 1:22-25

John opens his letter with profound intentionality.

> ¹ In the beginning was the Word, and the Word was with God, and the Word was God.

Take note that "Word" is capitalized for a reason. In the original Greek language, it is *Logos*. [11] Its original context means: "The Divine Expression, account, cause, or communication." [12]

So, therefore, when we get to verse 14 of chapter 1 and read:

> ¹⁴ The Word became flesh and made his dwelling among us. We have seen his glory, the glory of the one and only Son, who came from the Father, full of grace and truth.

What John is proclaiming to us is nothing short of incredible.

Jesus is the Word of God.

He is the Divine Expression, account, cause, or communication of God's glory, grace, truth, and love.

In fact, using substitution here, we could re-read John 1:1, combined with verse 14, to more fully understand John's message:

> In the beginning was Jesus, and Jesus was with God, and Jesus was God. God became flesh as Jesus Christ and made his dwelling among us. We have seen Jesus' glory, the glory of the one and only Son, who came from the Father, full of grace and truth.

This is pivotal to understand. The Divine Expression is God, and that Word is Jesus.

Therefore, from John, a first-person account of Jesus, we learn that Jesus is God in the flesh.

This is where John begins.

It is, therefore, where we also start.

Even if we were to stop here, in faith, I sincerely hope you see what I do. The Gospel message of John enables us to gain a deeper understanding that it is God Himself who dies for us on the cross and is resurrected as our hope of grace and truth.

If you step away from this book now, you can know this: in His love for us, God came to earth as Jesus Christ. This is not my words, but the Word of God, proclaimed by His disciples for us to wrestle with in our hearts and minds.

Light and Darkness

Let's continue through John's introduction of his letter by looking at verse 2. Here, John provides further explanation of the deity of Jesus Christ.

> ² He was with God in the beginning. ³ Through him all things were made; without him nothing was made that has been made. ⁴ In him was life, and that life was the light of all mankind. ⁵ The light shines in the darkness, and the darkness has not overcome it.

Here, the Greek Word for light or illumination is used. It is *phōs*, meaning "light," and it carries the context of illuminating truth. [13]

Phos, or light, is contrasted with the absence of light. The Greek word *skotia*, is translated as darkness. [14] It is a term used synonymously with moral and spiritual darkness apart from Christ.

Therefore, we could read verses 4 & 5 in a manner emphasizing this illumination of truth:

> ⁴ In [Jesus Christ] was life, and that life was the light [and illumination of truth for] all mankind. ⁵ The light [of God, Jesus Chrst,] shines in the [moral and spiritual] darkness, and the [moral and spiritual] darkness has not overcome it.

Don't miss this: John is making the point that Jesus is light in a world filled with moral depravity and spiritual darkness.

Next, if you follow along in chapter 1, John writes about that other John, John the Baptist. We will examine John the Baptist more closely in the next chapter as we delve into the second half of John 1. For now, just consider what John writes in verse 6.

> ⁶ There was a man sent from God whose name was John. ⁷ He came as a witness to testify concerning that light, so that through him all

might believe. [8] He himself was not the light; he came only as a witness to the light.

The point here is that John the Baptist, cousin of Jesus according to Luke's account, is not the Promised Messiah. He was a witness of Christ, the Promised Messiah. John the Baptist, however, was the prophesied foreteller of the coming of Christ.

Consider how verse 9 continues with the imagery of light proclaimed into a dark world.

> [9] The true light that gives light to everyone was coming into the world. [10] He [Jesus] was in the world, and though the world was made through him, the world did not recognize him. [11] He came to that which was his own, [meaning the people of God, the Jewish people] but his own did not receive him [The people of Israel rejected Jesus].

> [12] Yet to all who did receive him, to those who believed in his name, he gave the right to become children of God—[13] children born not of natural descent, nor of human decision or a husband's will, but born of God.

As John continues, he wants us to understand that the Promised Hope of the Messiah, who takes away the sins of the world and gives eternal hope to all people, is for all who believe in His name. All of us, no matter our origin, race, gender, identity, politics, past mistakes, absolutely ALL may be born again and become a part of God's family uniquely through Jesus.

Now, with this new context of who Jesus is and how He is light in the darkness, we can revisit verse 14. As you may recall from earlier, this passage helps us understand that Jesus is the *Logos*, the Word, and He is the beginning. The Word, God's Divine Expression, became flesh as Jesus and brought us the glory of God the Father.

Jesus brought light into our darkness.

Consider verse 14 once more.

> [14] The Word became flesh and made his dwelling among us. We have seen his glory, the glory of the one and only Son, who came from the Father, full of grace and truth.

> [15] (John [The Baptist] testified concerning him. He cried out, saying, "This is the one I spoke about when I said, 'He who comes after me has surpassed me because he was before me.' ") [16] Out of his fullness we have all received grace in place of grace already given. [17] For the law was given through Moses; grace and truth came through Jesus Christ. [18] No one has ever seen God, but the one and only Son, who is himself God and is in closest relationship with the Father, has made him known. [15]

This last part, verses 17 and 18, helps us understand why John, the writer of this gospel message, puts pen to paper. Law has been given, but "grace and truth" are revealed through Jesus Christ.

In verse 17, we see that the law, the legalistic constricting obsession of many, was in fact not the complete purpose of God. The Law only pointed us to the grace and truth of Jesus Christ.

Verse 18 then, quite bluntly, equates Jesus as God in the flesh. This bold proclamation of the deity of Jesus Christ is something worth pausing to consider for each of us. It's worth taking a little time to discuss what it means to you with your family, in a small group, or with your friends. It invites a deeper meditation.

For what we are invited to contemplate and to learn from these opening 18 verses of John's good news about Jesus has the power to completely change us. It upheaves our entire understanding of the world. It challenges us to initiate a revolutionary relationship with the God of all creation, one that reveals and deepens everything we have ever learned or experienced.

We learn from the first half of John's opening chapter that:

- The Word of God has always existed
- Jesus is God in the Flesh, a human being in our presence
- The hope and grace and truth of God came to us as the man Jesus Christ and, although the world is full of darkness, Jesus, the light and hope of God, overcame all darkness
- AND... finally... we learn that Jesus has made God the Father known to all the world and to us

Again, the final verse of John's opening prologue, John 1:18, says this:

> [18] No one has ever seen God, but the one and only Son, who is himself God and is in closest relationship with the Father, has made him known. [16]

John begins his message about Jesus by explaining that Jesus is God.

This leads us to a pivotal fact necessary to understanding Christianity.

There is one God.

This one God loved us so much that He appeared to us in the flesh as Jesus Christ.

To more fully understand this final sentiment in verse 18, let's look at one more Greek word. In the final part of verse 18, it says:

> ... the one and only son, who is himself God and is in closest relationship with the Father, has made him known.

Where the English translates "is in closest relationship with the Father," the Greek word used is *kolpos*. [17]

Kolpos literally means "bosom." In other words, "closest relationship with the Father" means internally a part of the Father. The words paint a vivid visual image here of a mother carrying a child in her bosom, although the word 'womb' is not used; instead, it is 'bosom'. Therefore, we are left to consider how Christ is not a separate thing that is delivered out of God; He is not parasitic like a child carried in the womb. It is more complete to understand that Jesus is much like the heart of God.

He is the internal, deepest part of God revealed to us through love.

Therefore, Jesus, the bosom of God, has exposed God's intent to us.

He is God's heart.

His arrival into our world brought God's light into our darkness.

2

God Is Here

John 1:19-51, Philippians 1:27-28 & Mark 1:16-20

John, son of a fisherman named Zebedee and an eyewitness to Jesus' life and ministry, proclaims loudly for all to hear: Jesus is God.

The writer of the Book of John announces to the world that God is here!

His opening words declare to us the power of grace, hope, and truth. The light of the world has come to break the chains of darkness for all who will believe in Him.

Jesus speaks into the darkness, holding the world in bondage, and His light destroys all fear and hate if we believe that God is here.

John's gospel goes all the way back to the genesis of all things.

John connects Christ, in the most plain terms, to God.

As he does, his readers receive this blasting truth of the deity of Christ. John retells the story of Jesus, and in its truth, we must all wrestle with the reality of a God who has become flesh for all. This theme of God's arrival becomes very important as we learn about Jesus' love, the love of God, and the light and hope of salvation.

Let's look at three things to take away from verses 19-51 of John 1. Actually, it's just one thing, but let's look at three things and conclude with the one.

It is Look, Come, Follow.

Look

In the previous chapter of this book, we addressed the authorship of the Book of John. We were able to clarify that it was not John the Baptist. However, John the Baptizer looms large in the narrative about Jesus in the fourth gospel account.

The Baptizing John is quite an interesting figure. Mark 1 describes him in this manner:

- He was a preacher
- His chief message was about life change
- He baptized people into repentance
- He wore a simple camel's hair garment with a leather belt around his waist
- He was said to live a simple life, eating locusts and wild honey

What a peculiar and different person.

You get the sense from reading the gospel accounts that John the Baptist was laser-focused on his mission. He rejects the comforts of this present world and lives in a manner that makes it possible for him to be a radically bold messenger of God.

John the Baptist, although he appears in the New Testament scriptures, is actually the last prophet of the Old Testament. We miss that sometimes when reading his narrative. His ministry comes and goes before the fulfillment of Jesus' death, burial, and resurrection. This places him within the period preceding Christ.

I like to imagine a red line representing the shed blood of Jesus separating all of creation. There is the time leading up to and before Jesus's atonement. Then there is all that comes afterwards. Like a red line separating all things, it also divides the Old and New Covenants from one another.

That red line is why we celebrate Easter.

It is the death of Jesus Christ.

It is the red line of His blood.

John the Baptist is born, preaches, and dies in that time before Jesus' death, and, therefore, he dies under the Old Covenant.

Still, why the emphasis on John the Baptist in all four of the gospel accounts?

John the Baptist is a type of messenger sent by God before Christ. He, like the Old Testament that his preaching represents, points us to Jesus. He points us to the promised redeemer from God.

In biblical times, when a person of great importance was traveling, heralds would precede them. They would, for example, tell people to get ready, something is about to happen. The king is passing through; look your best, be presentable. This provided a way for those along the king's path to show respect. It also provided an opportunity to honor, for example, the arrival of a conquering king or general. This would have been an important custom for helping to ensure the king thought well of you and your family.

Especially in Biblical times, it was not wise to offend those in authority.

A fun example of someone heralding the arrival of greatness can be seen in the Disney film *Aladdin*. After discovering the magic genie, Aladdin is made a prince of great wealth. When Prince Ali enters the city, what follows him is an entire parade and entourage. The Disney film has dancing monkeys, elephants, and acrobatic swordsmen. It's quite a spectacle; it demands that everyone take note of it.

This procession "heralds" and announces the arrival of someone important.

In our culture today, this still happens, but in a different format. It is certainly not as entertaining as having a magical genie dancing. When Presidents or other Heads of State travel, there is much pomp and circumstance. Someone goes ahead to ensure everything is ready. When they arrive, the red carpet is rolled out, the band plays, and cheering crowds gather.

Their arrival is heralded as a major event.

On a more personal level, our tradition of announcing the Bride and Groom at a wedding party reflects this same concept. Someone announces the newlyweds before they enter the reception. As they do, they are telling everyone, "Hey, look here, today is a day for these two happy people, get ready, welcome them, rejoice!"

In all of these cases, the person who goes before declares, "Get ready, pay attention, look your best. Don't miss this moment!"

Understanding this tradition is a good starting point for considering who John the Baptist is as a person. It even helps us to see why his message is important.

John the Baptist, again, is the prophesied foreteller of the coming Messiah.

His message is simple and clear. It is a message to all in his age and ours. John the Baptist comes before Jesus to foretell (or prophesy): "The King is coming, get ready, make straight the path!!"

This is what is going on in the second half of John chapter one.

John is interrogated about his identity. He replies with a denial about being the Messiah, Elijah, and the Prophet. After all of this, those questioning his identity demand an answer. John responds by referring to a prophecy from the Book of Isaiah.

He says, in verse 23 of John 1:

> [23] John replied in the words of Isaiah the prophet, "I am the voice of one calling in the wilderness, 'Make straight the way for the Lord.' "
> [18]

Considering the prophecy John the Baptist is referencing only helps to strengthen our faith. It is worth noting that Isaiah lived about 700 years before Jesus' birth. Yet, these words, written in Isaiah 40:1-5, powerfully foretell the purpose of John the Baptist.

[1] Comfort, comfort my people, says your God.

[2] Speak tenderly to Jerusalem,

and proclaim to her

that her hard service has been completed,

that her sin has been paid for,

that she has received from the Lord's hand

double for all her sins.

³ A voice of one calling:

"In the wilderness prepare

the way for the Lord;

make straight in the desert

a highway for our God. ᵇ

⁴ Every valley shall be raised up,

every mountain and hill made low;

the rough ground shall become level,

the rugged places a plain.

⁵ And the glory of the Lord will be revealed,

and all people will see it together.

For the mouth of the Lord has spoken." [19]

John makes it clear, in answering with a quote from Isaiah, that he is aware of his identity. He is not the Christ. He will not absorb the attention meant to be for Jesus.

He deflects all the attention to Christ. This reveals both his humility and makes him a good herald. Importantly, it reveals to us that he is the fulfillment of this prophecy.

John is the proclaimer.

He is the procession ahead of the King's arrival.

He is the one who goes ahead and prepares everyone for what is coming.

And his message remains poignant even today: "Get ready, God is here!"

Going back to John 1, this dialogue between John and the religious authorities confounds the stiff-necked, self-righteous leaders.

They want to know about John's authority to baptize. He says,

> [26] "I baptize with water," ..., "but among you stands one you do not know. [27] He is the one who comes after me, the straps of whose sandals I am not worthy to untie." [20]

Next, we read about John seeing Jesus arrive in the moment when He began His earthly ministry.

> [29] The next day John [again, this is John the Baptist] saw Jesus coming toward him and said, "Look, the Lamb of God, who takes away the sin of the world! [30] This is the one I meant when I said, 'A man who comes after me has surpassed me because he was before me.' [31] I myself did not know him, but the reason I came baptizing with water was that he might be revealed to Israel."

> [32] Then John gave this testimony: "I saw the Spirit come down from heaven as a dove and remain on him. [33] And I myself did not know him, but the one who sent me to baptize with water told me, 'The man on whom you see the Spirit come down and remain is the one who will baptize with the Holy Spirit.' [34] I have seen and I testify that this is God's Chosen One." [21]

Do you see what is going on here?

John the Baptist is pointing everyone's attention to the coming and promised Christ. He says, "Look." He points us all to behold this person we know today as Jesus.

John the Baptist declares, as each follower of Jesus should as well, that we must look to Jesus!

John the Baptist points people to look towards Jesus, and the Gospel of John points out that even his own followers begin to look to Jesus.

Come

Another point we can extract from the second half of John 1 comes from a key verb the author uses repeatedly.

It is the Greek verb *erchomai*. In English, it is translated as "to come or go (in a great variety of applications, literally and figuratively). It can be translated as "accompany, appear, bring, come, enter, fall out, go, and grow." [22] According to *A Concise Dictionary of the Words in the Greek Testament and The Hebrew Bible*, it is a verb that is only used in the present tense and the imperfect.

If you're like me and grew up hating grammar class, the imperfect tense refers to an incomplete action that began in the past. For example, "was walking" or "was arriving." Present, of course, refers to what is happening now. It is the tense we use when we say, "I walk" or "I arrive."

It is important to note here that *erchomai* conveys a sense of motion. It translates to English as "*I go...* or *I come.*" [23]

It conveys action.

If we thread all of John 1 together, using just this verb, it gives us a shortened message highlighting this powerful movement of God. It shows God's people in action.

Emphasis is added below to highlight where the verb erchomai has been translated.

⁷ He [John the Baptist]] **came** as a witness...

[that] ⁹ The true light that gives light to everyone **was coming** into the world.

¹¹ He **came** to that which was his own, but his own did not receive him.

John the Baptist then declares in verse 15:

... 'He who **comes** after me has surpassed me because he was before me.

And later in verse 27:
²⁷ He is the one who **comes** after me, the straps of whose sandals I am not worthy to untie.

Then, we come to verses 29-31:

²⁹ The next day John saw Jesus **coming** toward him and said, "Look, the Lamb of God, who takes away the sin of the world! ³⁰ This is the one I meant when I said, 'A man who **comes** after me has surpassed me because he was before me.' ³¹ I myself did not know him, but the reason I **came** baptizing with water was that he might be revealed to Israel." [24]

Threading this action together helps us to see a major theme beginning here and moving throughout the entire Book of John. In John's opening chapter, we start this vital eyewitness, authentic account of the life and teachings of Jesus Christ by learning two important things:

A) that Jesus is God and

B) God is here.

He has come to the Earth as it has been declared by the prophets of old, including John the Baptist.

The message is clear: our God **CAME** to us. He **COMES** to us still today. He meets us where we are with urgent and intentional purpose. To call us to "Follow Him."

Follow

To understand this final point, let's focus our attention on the final verses of John 1, verses 43-51.

Here, John reveals to us, his readers, why God has come to us.

John 1:43-51 is a powerful passage that reveals why Christ has come.

> [43] The next day Jesus decided to leave for Galilee. Finding Philip, he said to him, "Follow me."

Next, Philip finds Nathanael and tells him, in verse 45:

> "We have found the one Moses wrote about in the Law, and about whom the prophets also wrote—Jesus of Nazareth, the son of Joseph."

Nathanael replies with skepticism at the mention of where Jesus was from. His friend challenges the skeptic to have a look for himself.

Jesus identifies Nathanael as he is approaching and, in a manner left for us to ponder, convinces him that He is the Son of God. We see this in verse 49 and following:

> [49] ... Nathanael declared, "Rabbi, you are the Son of God; you are the king of Israel."

[50] Jesus said, "You believe because I told you I saw you under the fig tree. You will see greater things than that." [51] He then added, "Very truly I tell you, you will see 'heaven open, and the angels of God ascending and descending on' the Son of Man." [25]

Don't miss this: the message of Jesus, God in the flesh, the light of the world, the destroyer of darkness, is put to His disciples in the most straightforward manner possible. It is the same profound invitation He still extends to each of us today.

"Follow Me," beckons Jesus.

Jesus says, paraphrasing here, "I see you for who you are; yet, I have come to you, and I invite you to simply follow Me."

He repeats this invitation, a calling from God Himself, to "Follow" as He calls more of His disciples. Today, it remains an invitation from God for us to leave our old selves behind, be changed, and become more like Him.

Complete

In summary, the message that begins John's gospel is this: Look, Come, Follow. However, don't think of the call to "Follow" in the terms of our modern, social-media-obsessed world. Influencers on various platforms love this "follow me" language. We hear it every time we listen to a podcast. We see it on every short video or when we read a post or article.

"Like, follow, subscribe" is the language of our era.

These invitations are far different from those of Jesus. The influencer's invite implies a passive engagement or connection.

Yet, the message of Jesus Christ is not passive.

It is active.

It is profound.

God has come to us, for us.

He wants us to follow Him and be transformed.

He wants to change us.

This means, as followers of Jesus Christ, we are to continue actively pursuing ways to reach and save the lost. We are to engage in a process of transformation that beckons people to come to the light and to leave behind the darkness. The old is to be made new.

You and I must lean into each opportunity and every moment to answer the call to follow Jesus.

As His followers, may we, in everything we do, point people to "**Look**, to Jesus."

May we sound the call to the world, "**Come** and see."

And then, in the still moments when we experience Christ, when we truly connect with God, may we still hear His voice say, "**Follow** me."

Follow Me, Jesus calls, and we point others to find God.

Follow Me, Jesus invites, and come see how I will bless you.

Follow Me, Jesus beckons, and become love.

Jesus calls to us and says, simply, **"I see you. I know you. I love you... Follow Me."**

His disciples leave everything. They follow Him. He makes them complete.

May we ever do the same.

3

Room For Love

John 2:13-25

For Christians around the world, Ash Wednesday is a time of repentance. We pause to reflect on our mortality, then call out to God and ask His forgiveness for our sins. It is a reassurance of the forgiveness He has already granted. Ultimately, it is a time to rededicate ourselves to following Him.

The idea of repentance literally means to turn away from sin. It is the act of turning from our selfishness to following in the Way of Jesus. In simpler terms, it is the movement of our souls toward becoming selfless.

In following Jesus toward selflessness, we are transformed and changed from our former sense of being and purpose. We are born again and made new.

The receiving of ashes on Ash Wednesday reminds us of the spiritual death central to our turning away from our mistakes and fallenness. It is a powerfully symbolic moment.

In the act of repentance, we feel the weight of our guilt fall away.

We experience the joy of forgiveness and grace.

We begin to understand, if even only a little bit more, the absolute love of our God.

At the Temple

In John 2, we read a powerful story in which Jesus demonstrates the importance of cleansing through repentance.

Jesus goes to Jerusalem to celebrate the Jewish Passover. When He arrives there, He finds "people selling cattle, sheep and doves, and others sitting at tables exchanging money." [26] He drives them out of the temple courts, flipping their tables over in a dramatic moment that conveys anger.

At the temple, the center of Jewish worship, a place for repentance and acts of sincere devotion, Jesus witnesses corruption. It is a form of extortion that is occurring in the temple courts. Money changers were taking advantage of those on pilgrimage to worship and celebrate God in the Holy City. Essentially, these profiteers were using lies and deceit to profit from people with a sincere heart and a desire to make a sacrifice to the Lord.

Into this scene of corruption, walks Jesus.

To better understand what provokes Jesus to anger, let's put it into modern terms.

Imagine you go to your local church. As you approach the offering plate to present your tithe or offering, you are met by someone overseeing the donations. This person looks at your humble offering and, essentially, tells you your offering isn't good enough. For example, maybe the $20 bill you have is "Too old" to give to God.

"Surely," the moneychanger says as they offer an exchange, "This brand new, crisp, clean $20 bill will make a better offering."

Then, the corrupt individual sells you that $20 note for $30. They pocket the difference, profiting in their extortion and manipulation of someone's honest efforts to worship God.

In these terms, it becomes more clear what upset Jesus. It is corruption, and it is evil. Therefore, what we read about in John 2 is not an angry and vengeful God randomly trashing the temple courts. No, it is Jesus' righteous, wrathful judgment on behalf of love.

An outsider with no relationship to Jesus and no context would just see anger.

But, for those with a relationship with God, we can see it for what it is: it is justice. His immediate judgment was brought about by those who had chosen to do evil.

The important distinction we need to make here lies in the motivation behind Jesus' apparent anger. It is important because I've heard people take this story out of context to try and justify their anger. They might say, "My anger is ok because even Jesus got angry," or even "God gets angry sometimes."

To be clear, Jesus' violent overturning of the tables is not unjust. What happens in the temple courts is not the same as selfish human anger.

Human anger, or wrath, is born from hate, prejudice, selfishness, manipulative control, greed, and contempt. Human anger is unrighteous and unloving; it is selfish in nature.

By contrast, Jesus' violent actions demonstrate the righteous anger of God. It is a foreshadowing of His coming judgment upon those who do evil.

The Bible often employs descriptions of human emotions to convey the nature of God. We read phrases about God's wrath, God's anger, and even God's jealousy in the Scriptures. However, it is different in its motivation from human wrath, anger, and jealousy. It is selfless and not sinful.

Anger that is Godly and justified, what the Bible calls God's wrath and God's anger, can also be experienced by humans. It is what we experience when:

- We see the weak and helpless exploited.
- We see hypocrisy within the Church.
- We hear of someone's good works being criticized unjustly,

All of these things should provoke us to indignation. It should illicit a type of righteous anger that leaves us unsettled and moves us to act on behalf of those who are treated poorly.

It is the type of righteous anger we read about in the Bible.

Humans can experience the same type of holy, righteous indignation that Jesus Himself exhibits. However, it is not brash, and it should not provoke us to selfish action. When it does, it quickly devolves into sin.

When God is provoked to anger, it is on behalf of those He loves. It is always righteous moments of judgement that are not corrupted by selfishness.

Within Our Hearts

What, then, provokes Jesus to such anger in his flipping-the-tables moment? There are at least two reasons worth considering.

One, Jesus cares about the "why" of our worship. Jesus is not concerned with the outward appearance of our gifts or even the size of the gift. Jesus cares about our heart condition and the why behind our worship. In the temple courts, He is upset with the manipulation and chases those doing evil out of the sacred space. He chases them out of the temple area in dramatic fashion. Jesus makes it clear that the pure and simple way of giving sacrificially, with the proper motives, is the goal. He wants our "why" to be sincere devotion. He wants it to be love.

Secondly, we see Jesus cares about us as bearers of God's Light. To understand this, we need only to ask why the writer of John includes this story about cleaning the temple out. John could have left this account out of the story because it seems an inconvenient truth. It does, indeed, rub the casual reader the wrong way. However, for the person willng to look a little closer, it forces us to ask some difficult questions about the nature of God and the definition of love.

Here at the beginning of Jesus' ministry, Jesus has a moment of anger. While we can understand now why this happens, I think it is worth considering the author's objective in John's Gospel. I think the answer to the question of why it is included so early on in the story of Jesus helps the rest of this letter to take new significance.

Jesus is cleansing the temple, it is His Father's house, and it has been made corrupt.

In Genesis, we read that we, you and I, all of humanity, are, in fact, made in the image of God.

Genesis 1:26-27 says:

> [26] Then God said, "Let us make mankind in our image, in our likeness, so that they may rule over the fish in the sea and the birds in the sky, over the livestock and all the wild animals, and over all the creatures that move along the ground."

> [27] So God created mankind in his own image,

> in the image of God he created them;

male and female he created them. [27]

I believe John is reminding us that, as a result of Jesus' ministry and the gift of the Holy Spirit, we are also the temple of the Father. His Spirit lives in us. When we tolerate sin, we are defiling the holy space where God indwells us.

Jesus, in His absolute love for us, wants to clean out the corruption hidden in our hearts.

If we are to follow this line of thought, we can re-read John 2 and imagine what Jesus might say to us as we come to terms with our need for repentance and cleansing.

Imagine, for a moment, that the temple courts are your soul. They represent the inner part of your self, the part where you invited the Holy Spirit to dwell when you accepted Christ as your Savior.

Jesus walks into the temple of your heart. He steps into this holy chamber.

If we imagine this scene, and then creatively rewrite John 2, it takes on a much more personal tone.

> When it was time, Jesus was made known to us. In the courts of our hearts, however, he found greed, lust, corruption, selfishness, evil, hate, anger, hypocrisy, and all manner of sin. It was present and tolerated in the holy place of our heart. The very place we had invited Him to dwell.

> So he fashioned a tool by which to drive out all sin and evil from within us. Similar to flipping the tables of a money changer, Jesus destroyed the instruments and mechanisms by which we are continually enslaved to our selfishness.

To those trapped in addiction: to their selfishness, to substances, to vanity, to judgmental attitudes, to arrogance, to pride, to bigotry and indifference, to all people overcoming all manner of sin, Jesus spoke. He said, "Get these out of here! Stop turning my Father's house into a place profiting from the divisiveness of sin and corruption!" [28]

When we take this more personal approach to imagining the story of Jesus happening inside our own hearts, it gives new meaning to how his disciples remark about His zeal for the house of the Lord!

His anger is provoked by His sincere attempts to protect us in His perfect love.

Here, then, is the bottom line: Jesus wants to come into the temple of our hearts, into the most sacred, God-created center of our existence, and make us new again. He wants to purge the evil and make us clean.

However, He is no tyrant. We must invite Him in and allow Him to change us from the inside out.

Ash Wednesday is about remembering our need for repentance. It is a reminder that we must die to ourselves and a somber look at our mortality.

Before we meet that end, however, we are invited by God to allow Him to transform us from the inside out.

Will you welcome His cleansing of you from the inside out?

Will you repent and turn back to Him?

Will you make room in your heart for His perfect love?

4

Love Is Here

John 3

John 3 begins by introducing us to a man named Nicodemus, who was a Pharisee and a member of the Jewish ruling council. Who is Nicodemus, and what does his interaction with Jesus teach us about love?

To begin with, Nicodemus is a highly respected leader in his community. He is part of the council that rules the Jews and provides leadership for them based on their Old Testament Law. In this sense, Nicodemus, we could say, is a representative of man's best understanding of how to live out the Law of God as given to us through Moses. He represents the embodiment of a legalistic approach to interacting with our Creator.

Secondly, we read in verse 2 that Nicodemus "came to Jesus at night..." This does not mean he is necessarily ashamed of going to see Jesus. It is more likely just an opportune time for them to sit and discuss heavy matters without the distraction of the crowds being around. Yet, the fact that Nicodemus, a teacher of the Old Law, is coming to Jesus at night bears at least some metaphorical significance.

These two things combine to give us a better understanding of Nicodemus and insight into why John includes his inquisitive story in his accounting of Jesus' life.

Nicodemus is, both literally and figuratively, in the dark seeking the light. As a person who has studied the Old Law, he remains in the dark.

In the darkness, at night, he seeks out Jesus, the light.

His knowledge, as a well-studied teacher of the Old Law and legalism, has not created light within him. It has, however, pointed towards the light now appearing in the darkness.

The imagery of light coming into the world is a major theme of John's testimony concerning Jesus, and we'd be amiss to not revisit it here.

Again, Nicodemus, a teacher of the Old Law, someone who holds others accountable to the Old Testament legalism, is in the dark, seeking the One who is Light.

Don't miss that because it is incredibly important to understand.

Remember how John began his account of Jesus' ministry. This is John 1:1-5:

> [1] In the beginning was the Word, and the Word was with God, and the Word was God. [2] He was with God in the beginning. [3] Through him all things were made; without him nothing was made that has been made. [4] In him was life, and that life was the light of all mankind. [5] The light shines in the darkness, and the darkness has not overcome it. [29]

The "light" is Jesus, and, as we will see, that light is sacrificial and absolute love for all people!

Ok, back to John 3. In verse 3, we read Jesus' response to Nicodemus' statement about Jesus being "a teacher who has come from God" because of the signs He has performed. [30] Jesus then replies, in verse 3:

> ³ ... "Very truly I tell you, no one can see the kingdom of God unless they are born again."

Nicodemus takes this literally; he is perhaps focusing on the nature of inheritance as a person born into the nation of Israel. Nicodemus is imagining a physical rebirth, and it baffles him.

Puzzled, he responds to Jesus:

> ⁴ "How can someone be born when they are old?" Nicodemus asked. "Surely they cannot enter a second time into their mother's womb to be born!" [31]

Birthright

Now, I have heard many preachers stumble around this message and assume the physicality of an adult being reborn is what shocks Nicodemus. Sure, that could be the case. It is, after all, a shocking and altogether disgusting thing to imagine. Childbirth is gross enough, but to imagine a full-grown person born from their mother's womb as an adult is bizarre. To limit Nicodemus, a very respected and learned man, in his thinking to this base idea, seems to be missing the point.

If we make that physicality our only focus, we also miss the point, and it threatens to insult our intelligence. While the spiritual "rebirth" is a metaphor that yields many puns, none of them convey the message of love that God is communicating here.

When we remember that Nicodemus is an Old Testament legal expert, it sheds more depth on this dialogue. He is thinking of the Law in the most concrete terms. The teacher of the Old Law knows how it places an emphasis on one's birth as a type of right. The order and nature of one's birth implies even a type of privileged access into the Kingdom of God as a descendant of Abraham, the Father of Judaism. I think Nicodemus, when he stumbles around about being physically reborn, is concerned with the Laws concerning birthright.

In Nicodemus' legalistic understanding of his time:

- One becomes a member of the nation of Israel primarily based on the identity of their birth parents.
- They were given certain legal rights and inheritance based on the nature of their birth order.
- An individual was born into a covenantal or contractual relationship with God, a birthright that meant they were set apart from the rest of the world.

This is sometimes complicated for us to understand in our modern era. The concept of birthright is somewhat foreign to us. In America, as in much of the Western world, we grow up believing that anyone can overcome the circumstances of their birth. We have embraced the idea that your birthright, while it can certainly benefit or harm you, is not what defines you.

The Old Law differs significantly from this concept. You were either Jewish, a member of the nation of Israel by right of your birth; or you were a gentile person, a non-Jew.

Therefore, what Nicodemus is wrestling with, in his exchange with Jesus, is less the physical birth and more the birthright. It is the idea of breaking away from the legal notion that your parents, your heritage, your ancestry, are your primary God-given connection to your spiritual identity. The nation of God's people, in this case based on the Old Law, often excluded outsiders and was prone to judging others in a legalistic manner.

Teaching the teacher

From this patriarchal, highly structured, legalistic understanding, Jesus begins to teach the teacher. Verse 5 of John 3 records Jesus' response to Nicodemus:

> [5] Jesus answered, "Very truly I tell you, no one can enter the kingdom of God unless they are born of water and the Spirit. [6] Flesh gives birth to flesh, but the Spirit gives birth to spirit. [7] You should not be surprised at my saying, 'You must be born again.' [32]

Then, we can imagine these men sitting around a fire at night discussing these important matters. Perhaps a wind rustles the trees in the darkness. Maybe it licks the fire and kicks up the embers or blows the smoke amongst them for a moment. They hear the wind. They witness the surrounding trees bow under the pressure of the moving air.

Jesus, then says, in verse 8:

> [8] The wind blows wherever it pleases. You hear its sound, but you cannot tell where it comes from or where it is going. So it is with everyone born of the Spirit." [33]

Nicodemus leans in for more information. He, like any good teacher, asks good questions. He wants to understand the meaning of Jesus' words.

As he inquires for more information, Jesus calls back to a moment in Israel's history when God provided a rather foolish-looking monument for people to look upon to be healed. Jesus references Moses lifting up a snake in the wilderness as an act of national repentance. [34]

In that wilderness moment from the past, the faith of God's people required them to trust God and humble themselves. Those who were saved turned away from their pride. They looked, in faithful obedience, to God's provided plan of redemption. They looked up, even though it seemed a foolish thing to do.

Those who obeyed were healed.

Next, in John's gospel, we read what is considered to be the most famous passage of all the Bible: John 3:16.

Now, it is important to note that this is the writer of John explaining to us what Jesus has just said. If you have a red-letter Bible, you'll note these words are not in red. They are not spoken by Jesus. Yet, they are a powerful proclamation about Jesus from someone who sat at His feet learning from Him day and night.

John 3:16 is the powerful teaching we are to take away from this passage. It is born out of Jesus' ministry, and this moment John is recounting for us. The writer of John pens these divinely inspired words. As they do, it reveals to us both the nature of Jesus and the purpose of His ministry on Earth.

> [16] For God so loved the world that he gave his one and only Son, that whoever believes in him shall not perish but have eternal life. [35]

It is a profound and simple declaration of God's love for all people.

Immediately, John then provides clarification to teach us how God's Son is not here for condemnation, He is for salvation. It clearly lays out the difference between the former Old Law and its fulfillment in the new teachings of Jesus. It is a contrast between the legalistic world of the church-insiders, like Nicodemus, to the grace-filled, love-giving ministry of Jesus Christ. It is a contrast between dark and light.

Verse 17 proclaims that God's message of love is the absolute goal.

[17] For God did not send his Son into the world to condemn the world, but to save the world through him. [18] Whoever believes in him is not condemned, but whoever does not believe stands condemned already because they have not believed in the name of God's one and only Son. [36]

It's worth noting that the Greek word used here for "Whoever" literally means "every kind of, everyone, all people." [37]

It is an all-encompassing invitation to all who will believe.

John teaches us, as Jesus teaches the teacher, that God's love is for everyone.

Jesus, therefore, makes it clear that it is not your birth order, birthright, nationality, gender, wealth, denomination, political affiliation, nor sinful history that is central to the message of Jesus. It is none of that. None of it separates anyone from God, ever.

For the one who believes, God's message of love frees us of judgment and connects us to the eternal blessing of God through Jesus Christ.

Very Truly

John continues to drive home his point by contrasting light and darkness.

He declares, again, that light has come.

Then, he explains to us that some people loved the darkness, or the old ways, more than the light, or the love of God shining through Jesus. He even contrasts those who fear to come into the light because of their evil deeds with those who seek the truth and a relationship with God. [38]

Lastly, to bring us to the point at the end of John 3, we read this summary from John, the writer of the Book of John, revealing the central importance of Jesus Christ.

Thes final verses add clarity to emphasize John's point here. As you read John 3:31-36, take special note of the words in the brackets. They help to highlight and add clarity to John's message about Jesus.

> ³¹ The one who comes from above [Jesus] is above all; the one who is from the earth belongs to the earth, and speaks as one from the earth. The one who comes from heaven [Jesus] is above all. ³² He [Jesus] testifies to what he [Jesus] has seen and heard, but no one accepts his [Jesus'] testimony. ³³ Whoever has accepted it has certified that God is truthful. ³⁴ For the one whom God has sent [Jesus] speaks the words of God, for God gives the Spirit without limit. ³⁵ The Father loves the Son [Jesus] and has placed everything in his hands. [in Jesus' hands] ³⁶ Whoever believes in the Son [Jesus] has eternal life, but whoever rejects the Son [Jesus] will not see life, for God's wrath remains on them. [39]

Jesus as the fulfillment of the Old Law and as the light of God, shining in the darkness, is central to John's message.

Okay, great. What do we do with this?

Additionally, in John 3, there are two verses that reveal much to us about the Christian faith.

Consider John 3, verse 3 and verses 5-6, below.

John 3:3:

> ³ Jesus replied, "Very truly I tell you, no one can see the kingdom of God unless they are born again." [40]

John 3:5-6:

> [5] Jesus answered, "Very truly I tell you, no one can enter the kingdom of God unless they are born of water and the Spirit. [6] Flesh gives birth to flesh, but the Spirit gives birth to spirit. [41]

This phrase, "very truly," is translated from the Greek word: *amēn*, and it shows up 99 times in the New Testament. [42]

The Greek *amēn* is the word translated to "Amen." It is what we say at the end of a prayer. When we do, we are saying, "So be it," or "We agree," or "We are in agreement." It is a moment of unity.

However, here in these two verses and many other times, Jesus says "*amēn*" at the beginning of a statement. The difference in meaning is profound.

When you read your Bible and come across a statement by Jesus that begins with "Very truly" or "Verily, verily" or "Truly, truly," it is this amēn statement. It is translated into English in all of those ways. What we need to understand is that Jesus, saying this word at the beginning of a phrase, is Him making a statement of truth that is irrefutable.

It has a greater meaning than a pledge or an oath.

Jesus saying, "*amēn*" at the beginning of a statement has the weight of a legal testimony of fact.

It is the truth as accounted for by an eyewitness.

It is as absolute, as if the king of a nation witnessed a crime and declared judgment.

It is a statement that is irrefutable on the authority of the speaker.

Therefore, we do well to take note when Jesus says such things.

Here in John 3:3 & 5-6, if we paraphrase Jesus, He is saying: "This is an irrefutable fact, you must be born again to see the kingdom of God, and you can not enter the kingdom of God unless you are born again." [43]

And in both of these cases, Jesus proclaims not just hope and love; it is a message that saves all people. Specifically, He tells us that we may be changed from the inside out in a type of re-birth that aligns our internal, eternal, and innermost essence to the Spirit of the Living God.

This is the message at the root of Christianity.

It is the transformation that occurs within us when we invite God to make us new again.

This is the message each and every one of us must commit to at once and recommit to daily as we, in each moment, seek to become ambassadors or representatives of God's Kingdom.

In this declaration of truth from Jesus, we learn to:

- Shed our selfishness
- Reject holier-than-thou righteousness
- Submit to God alone

We welcome Jesus Christ into our hearts and find complete and total transformation.

We are, very truly, born again into His perfect love.

5

Labelled With Love

John 4 - 6 & Psalm 32:1-5

¹ Blessed is the one whose transgression is forgiven,
   whose sin is covered.
   ² Blessed is the man against whom the Lord counts no iniquity,
   and in whose spirit there is no deceit.
   ³ For when I kept silent, my bones wasted away
   through my groaning all day long.
   ⁴ For day and night your hand was heavy upon me;
   my strength was dried up as by the heat of summer. *Selah*
   ⁵ I acknowledged my sin to you,
   and I did not cover my iniquity;
   I said, "I will confess my transgressions to the Lord,"
   and you forgave the iniquity of my sin. *Selah* [44]
   - Psalm 32:1-5

We live in an era where people are all to often obsessed with labels.

We obsess over affiliation, pronouns, gender, and bias. We concern ourselves with the polar opposites of political correctness or staunch alignment with our own values. This socially acceptable judgementalism, dragging people to extreme perspectives, serves as an ever-deepening divide.

The tension is palpable.

Our news media organizations and politicians have figured out how impassioned these topics are to those who are willing to engage in such blatant attacks on normalism. So, they trumpet their perspective and rally people around labels. Their success gets them more attention. The attention, spreading like wildfire, gives rise to ever more labels and an endless tearing down of civility. Meanwhile, the voices at the center of these debates increase their ratings.

These attempts to label one another, or to take on a label defining ourselves, are not a new invention. It is as old as humanity itself. In its primitive form, it would have looked like tribalism. In our more connected modern era, we seem to have reverted to a neo-tribalism based on misguided labels.

If labels have always existed in some form or another, it is worth asking:

What does the Bible tell us about the labels we put on ourselves?

What does it teach us about the labels we place on one another?

Should we obsess over such labels?

Labelmaker

The concept of label-making is not new; in fact, it has always been used to help reveal what is hidden. Labels allow us to identify things and their value.

My wife loves to organize things. She is, to be honest, much better at it than I am.

A few years ago, she purchased a simple device called a "labelmaker." You have probably seen some version of the same thing. They are extremely useful for communicating the identity of items hidden in boxes on the top shelf of the pantry or in the clutter-filled attic spaces of our homes.

Labelmakers provide a tool for communicating something's identity, even when it seems hidden to us.

In the opening chapters of John's Gospel, the writer routinely pulls out the labelmaker and affixes words of identification to Jesus. The labels placed on Jesus equate Him with God.

John labels Jesus as the Creator.

Jesus is labelled as the promised Messiah.

Jesus is Lord.

Jesus is the Redeemer.

Jesus is God.

Jesus is love.

In chapters 4, 5, and 6, the writer of John continues a logical progression of John the Baptist's testimony concerning Jesus' divine origin. In doing so, we learn about our need to believe in Him for salvation.

As we learn about the labels attached to Jesus, the labels revealing what had previously been hidden, we also learn about the labels we have placed on ourselves and others. In John 4-6, the writer of John displays some of the ways Jesus specifically speaks into this uncertain world, offering a solution for all people. The message here is an overwhelming testimony of God's complete provision of love, grace, and mercy for all people.

It is love for ALL people.

We are labelled as "loved" despite our past decisions and present situations.

This begs a question: "Why does John highlight these specific instances of Jesus' ministry?"

It is essential to remember that John does not record every single thing he witnessed Jesus do. His gospel letter is not all-encompassing. It is not intended to be. It is, itself, like a label used to highlight the most important things.

It is meant to reveal to us what we might have missed.

We know this to be the case, not because it is some magical interpretation of the Scriptures. No, we know it because the writer tells us as much.

In John 21:25, we read these words:

> [25] Jesus did many other things as well. If every one of them were written down, I suppose that even the whole world would not have room for the books that would be written. [45]

Therefore, when we read John's testimony concerning Jesus' life, it is worth our pausing to lean in and reflect on the "Why?"

Why did the writer feel a need to include these specific stories? Answering this question helps us see the importance of what we are reading.

Like labels indicating what is hidden in a box in the closet, these words are meant to communicate to us what happened that is most important.

They invite a deeper study into the relationship offered with God through Jesus Christ.

Unlike our very uncertain and challenging world, a place where we only seem to be offered further division and confusion, Jesus provides certainty. Jesus offers relief from life's trials.

He gives us an eternal perspective that should profoundly change us. It is an invitation to be changed from the inside out.

Radical Labels

As John highlights teachings from Jesus that help us to see the eternal perspective of God's love for us, we begin to see them connected to our needs. In each case, John focuses on Jesus' teachings using elements and things we all require to exist and thrive.

These felt needs of all humanity become labels to communicate God's love.

For example, we see these elements related to human existence as presented in John's gospel:

- Water - for those who thirst in John 4
- Health - for those who are unwell in John 4 & 5
- Food - for those who hunger in John 4, 5, & 6
- Peace - for those who are anxious in John 4 & 6

These all permeate our human experience as necessary.

To emphasize this point, consider how:

- The lack of water leads to death by thirst.
- The lack of health is illness and suffering.
- The lack of food leads to hunger and starvation.

- Finally, the lack of peace is war.

Our human existence is often defined and labelled by the presence or lack of these essential things.

Furthermore, as Jesus points out in His teachings, we often go beyond labeling things and concepts; we also label one another. We use labels such as alien, criminal, enemy, addict, or outsider to label someone as unwanted or less-than.

To these people, Jesus says, "Come in."

To the downtrodden, poor, anxious, ill, worthless, and weak, Jesus says, "I'll lift you up."

To the hungry and desperate, He says, "Be filled."

To the thirsty, He says, "Be satisfied and never thirst again."

All of these classifications, human-based labels, account for how we judge other people. It leads to divisiveness and cruelty. In our world, the thirsty, the anxious, the ill, the hungry, and all who are outsiders get labeled as insufficient or unworthy.

God says, "No, that is not the case."

"You are worthy of My love."

John highlights the radical way that Jesus not only embraces those in need, but also provides for them mercy and grace. He radically labels all of humanity as worthy of His forgiveness and love.

New Water

If we dig into the text, we see Jesus' radical love come to life through John's accounting of His life.

In John 4, Jesus uses the concept of thirst to make a powerful point about His love for outsiders.

Beginning with verse four, we begin to read:

> [4] Now he [Jesus] had to go through Samaria. [5] So he came to a town in Samaria called Sychar, near the plot of ground Jacob had given to his son Joseph. [6] Jacob's well was there, and Jesus, tired as he was from the journey, sat down by the well. It was about noon.
>
> [7] When a Samaritan woman came to draw water, Jesus said to her, "Will you give me a drink?" [46]

Here, Jesus meets a Samaritan woman at the well outside the city.

Important to understand this story is the fact that they are drawing from "Jacob's well." The setting of this dramatic interaction between Jesus and the Samaritan woman at this specific well helps us realize that Jesus is not only talking about liquid water. Rather, He is providing a continuation of the comparison the writer used in John chapter 3.

If you recall, from the early chapter, we discussed Nicodemus. He was the teacher of the Old Testament law who was seeking light in the darkness. His seeking leads him to Jesus.

Here in John 4, Jacob's Well also originates from the Old Testament. It carries the same powerful symbolism as seen in John 3, where Jesus steps into an explanation and fulfillment of the Old Testament.

Jesus meets this woman at the Old Well, which was provided by her ancestors.

He then begins to teach about how He is bringing something new on a deeper spiritual level.

As He does, he is also referring to the ancient traditions connected to the Old Law.

Just as Nicodemus experienced the light in the darkness, here the woman at the well discovers thirst-quenching love as it is redefined.

We do not know the name of the woman Jesus meets with, but from John's account, we can learn a few key things about her.

First off, she is out getting water in the middle of the day. It was more common to fetch water in the early morning hours before the heat of the day arrived. It would have been a social gathering for the more respected women of the village. The timing of her visit to the well suggests she doesn't want to be fetching water when the other women are at the well. She sees herself as an outsider.

We see why when she interacts with Jesus. She is abrasive, and her interactions are, at best, stand-offish.

From her conversation with Christ, we also learn that she has been married multiple times. She is divorced. In the culture she lives in, the circumstances would not have mattered concerning her separation from various men. The fact that she has been married, more than once, implies the fault is largely hers. It might be that she just couldn't produce a child and has been cast aside; that was a harsh reality for many women in ancient times. However, it could also be something more sinister.

Her numerous broken relationships may indicate that she was not suited for family life. Alternatively, it is possible that she could have simply been the victim of bad marriages. We don't really know what led to her sense of brokenness. What we do know is what is implied; she is labelled as an outsider and unwanted.

The implications here are devastating. She is either quite a terrible person or just unable to function well within the norms of society.

While I personally think it is a gross exaggeration based on oversimplification, we should acknowledge that some have gone so far as to label her a harlot.

Call her what you will.

Label her as you would like.

This lady is an outsider.

She is an outcast, and she knows it.

Jesus, as we see in the following verses, steps into her broken world and invites her to reject that label of outcast. He calls her to tear off the world's labels and to be changed.

This woman is going to Jacob's well to draw water. She is in the middle of an act symbolic of seeking life in the old ways and patterns of the world. Jesus arrives and gives her living water.

In the next verses of John 4, she is confrontational with Jesus. She asks Jesus if He is somehow greater than the ones who passed this well down from ancient times. His response, recorded for us in John 4:13-14, is powerful.

> [13] Jesus answered, "Everyone who drinks this water will be thirsty again, [14] but whoever drinks the water I give them will never thirst. Indeed, the water I give them will become in them a spring of water welling up to eternal life." [47]

As a result of Jesus' calling, the woman leaves behind her jars for fetching the old water. She abandons the tools and trappings of her old life. Then, she goes to tell people about this new, eternal, life-giving well from which we are all invited to drink.

She begins something new.

She, the outcast, is changed by the water offered by Jesus.

She, the outsider, allows His message of unconditional love to well up inside of her.

She, the offensive and hurt woman, becomes a source of hope for those around her.

She embraces her new label. She is labelled with love.

New Life

Jumping forward a few verses. We read in 4:43-54 of an important person coming to Jesus to heal his sick child. The second part of verse 46, and following, tells us:

> 46 ... And there was a certain royal official whose son lay sick at Capernaum. 47 When this man heard that Jesus had arrived in Galilee from Judea, he went to him and begged him to come and heal his son, who was close to death. [48]

This person is anxious, scared, and worried. Anyone who has ever kept watch beside their sick child's bed, despairing over their health, knows how this unnamed person must have felt.

Desparation for healing is a human condition we can all empathize with, especially when it concerns one of our children.

Yet, Jesus speaks a word, and the child is healed from afar.

In verse 50, we read:

> 50 "Go," Jesus replied, "your son will live."
>
> The man took Jesus at his word and departed. [49]

Jesus speaks, and anxiety is gone.

Don't miss this: He creates immediate peace for those who place their faith in Him.

In chapter five, we read about an invalid man sitting by a pool. He is languishing. This begins in verse three:

> ³ Here [at this pool of water,] a great number of disabled people used to lie—the blind, the lame, the paralyzed. ⁵ One who was there had been an invalid for thirty-eight years. ⁶ When Jesus saw him lying there and learned that he had been in this condition for a long time, he asked him, "Do you want to get well?"

⁷ "Sir," the invalid replied, "I have no one to help me into the pool when the water is stirred. While I am trying to get in, someone else goes down ahead of me." [50]

The English word used to label people as "disabled" and "invalid" is translated from a Greek word meaning sickness or weakness. It "refers to a disability, often due to natural limitations or illness." [51]

It implies someone labeled by the outward brokenness of their condition.

From the man's interaction with Jesus, we get the sense that he is completely defeated and despairing. Powerless, he has surrendered to the label this world has placed upon him.

While the exact nature of his illness is unknown, it is also not the point here. The man is looking for a way to get well physically; however, his mind is so defeated he just passively sits there. He has given up. His struggle has grown to be as much about self-apathy as it is physical infirmity.

I think that is why the writer uses the Greek word *astheneia*. [52]

The man is sick and weak.

The world has cast him aside.

We can imagine the labels placed on him. If he were alive today, there might be those who would bully or take advantage of such a person due to his weakness.

By contrast, Jesus sees the broken and changes the labels applied to him. We read about this in verse 8:

> [8] Then Jesus said to him, "Get up! Pick up your mat and walk." [9] At once the man was cured; he picked up his mat and walked. [53]

Jesus says to the man labelled by the world as unworthy: "Those labels have no power over you, be healed, be whole."

Of course, Jesus' healing this man on the Sabbath creates a confrontation with the legalistic and self-righteous religious leaders of His day.

When they confront Him, Jesus responds with authority.

Label Changer

Previously, we talked about this phrase, "Very truly." It is translated from the Greek word: *amēn*, and it shows up 99 times in the New Testament. As a reminder, *amēn*, is the word translated to "Amen" that you and I say at the end of a prayer. When we do, we are in unity saying, "So be it," or "We agree," or "We are in agreement." It is a moment of unity. [54]

However, Jesus says "*amēn*" at the beginning of a statement, and the difference is profound.

Jesus is making a statement of truth that is irrefutable.

It is undeniable.

It would be akin to the eyewitness account of an absolute monarch, a king of a nation, being brought into court during ancient times.

There is no cross-examination needed.

This statement is a fact.

Amēn appears several times in John 5.

Here are Jesus' words in John 5:19:

> [19] Jesus gave them this answer: "Very truly I tell you, the Son can do nothing by himself; he can do only what he sees his Father doing, because whatever the Father does the Son also does. [20] For the Father loves the Son and shows him all he does. Yes, and he will show him even greater works than these, so that you will be amazed. [21] For just as the Father raises the dead and gives them life, even so the Son gives life to whom he is pleased to give it. [22] Moreover, the Father judges no one, but has entrusted all judgment to the Son, [23] that all may honor the Son just as they honor the Father. Whoever does not honor the Son does not honor the Father, who sent him. [55]

Next, in verse 24, we read:

> [24] "Very truly I tell you, whoever hears my word and believes him who sent me has eternal life and will not be judged but has crossed over from death to life. [56]

There is another such statement for us to consider beginning in verse 25:

[25] Very truly I tell you, a time is coming and has now come when the dead will hear the voice of the Son of God and those who hear will live. [26] For as the Father has life in himself, so he has granted the Son also to have life in himself. [27] And he has given him authority to judge because he is the Son of Man. [57]

These statements make a loud proclamation.

Jesus labels Himself as directly connected to the Father.

Jesus labels His Words as essential.

Jesus labels His authority as eternal.

John continues to lay out more of Jesus' teachings. Within this same section of Scripture, Jesus again confronts the legalistic mindset of the Old Testament-based religous leaders.

His message resounds, "I am bringing something new from out of the old."

Christ references Moses. As He does, He evokes a powerful comparison highlighting the deeper implications of the two label-breaking miracles He performs in chapter 6.

If you recall the Exodus story, under Moses, the people were provided with quail and manna through a miraculous provision of God. [58] Jesus' miracle of feeding the five thousand in the first half of John 6 replicates, in a dramatic call back to Exodus, a humble offering. God provided for all of the gathered people a feast of bread and fish when they sought Him for help.

They are labelled as hungry, and He feeds them.

Then, also in the first half of John 6 and in contrast to God parting the Red Sea for the people to follow Moses to the Promised Land, Jesus simply walks across the water. [59]

The people are labelled as desperate, and He comforts them.

Jesus changes the labels from old to new.

Where Moses' Old Testament faith provided daily rations, Jesus gives a feast.

Where Moses' Old Testament dividing of the water provided passage, Jesus overcomes and walks above the water. He conquers the storms. He speaks, and the very waves and winds obey.

Jesus is above all.

Again, the writer of John is highlighting these moments to show us, his readers, that Jesus is greater than the Old Law. It is an ongoing theme, and it gets driven home as we look at a few more of the *"amēn"* statements of Jesus. [60] The rest of chapter 6 is chock-full of more dynamic statements of truth from Jesus.

> 26 ... "Very truly I tell you, you are looking for me, not because you saw the signs I performed but because you ate the loaves and had your fill. 27 Do not work for food that spoils, but for food that endures to eternal life, which the Son of Man will give you. For on him God the Father has placed his seal of approval." [61]

> 32 ... "Very truly I tell you, it is not Moses who has given you the bread from heaven, but it is my Father who gives you the true bread from heaven. 33 For the bread of God is the bread that comes down from heaven and gives life to the world." [62]

[35]... Then Jesus declared, "I am the bread of life. Whoever comes to me will never go hungry, and whoever believes in me will never be thirsty. [63]

[47] Very truly I tell you, the one who believes has eternal life. [48] I am the bread of life. [49] Your ancestors ate the manna in the wilderness, yet they died. [50] But here is the bread that comes down from heaven, which anyone may eat and not die. [51] I am the living bread that came down from heaven. Whoever eats this bread will live forever. [64]

Jesus is using symbolic imagery to teach. He is using language to get the attention of the legalistic Jews who are obsessed with the things of this world. As He does, He is also making a division between the labels and ideas of the spiritual world versus the traps of focusing only on the physical world.

To emphasize this point, consider John 6:53-58:

[53] Jesus said to them, "Very truly I tell you, unless you eat the flesh of the Son of Man and drink his blood, you have no life in you. [54] Whoever eats my flesh and drinks my blood has eternal life, and I will raise them up at the last day. [55] For my flesh is real food and my blood is real drink. [56] Whoever eats my flesh and drinks my blood remains in me, and I in them. [57] Just as the living Father sent me and I live because of the Father, so the one who feeds on me will live because of me. [58] This is the bread that came down from heaven. Your ancestors ate manna and died, but whoever feeds on this bread will live forever." [65]

Finally, at the end of chapter 6, we read the response to Jesus' teaching. We learn that His challenge for us to change from our Old ways causes many to turn away from Him. They simply refuse to break the labels and accept the new ones.

Jesus, however, is redefining the labels a broken world puts on imperfect people. One would think people would be happy and joyful about such a freeing change. It is rejected by many, and John tells us that His radical, label-changing, all-accepting message causes many to stop following Him. They reject Jesus and His teachings.

Labelled with Love?

For us today, as an application, I would just ask you to consider verse 68 at the end of John chapter 6. Here, the writer records the faithful response of Jesus' disciples as so many turn away from Him.

> [68] Simon Peter answered him, "Lord, to whom shall we go? You have the words of eternal life. [69] We have come to believe and to know that you are the Holy One of God." [66]

Here, then, is the choice each of us is confronted with when we study the love of God. Jesus invites us into a relationship that requires us to make a decision.

Will we accept His labels over us as more important and defining than those of this world?

In every situation, Jesus speaks to the heart of the matter. He looks past the labels people have placed over themselves and way beyond the labels society has put on them. Jesus rejects the labels of the world.

For the woman at the well, labeled an outcast and worse, she is dry and thirsting for something real and lasting. Jesus heals her broken heart. He invites her to drink the everlasting water of redemption.

Over her life, Jesus speaks the label of love. He welcomes her into the living water drawn from the everlasting well.

To the person filled with worry over their sick child, labelled as despairing and anxious, Jesus speaks into the moment and heals them. He frees them from anxiety.

Over this person and their family, Jesus speaks the label of love as He provides peace.

Into the apathetic and despairing life of the disabled person who has given up on life, labelled as less-than and as unclean and as worthless, Jesus heals. He eliminates the self-centered affliction, reigniting passion and faith.

Over the lame man, Jesus speaks the label of love, and He walks away from despair.

In every case, just like in the story of the feeding of the 5,000, Jesus meets our exact needs.

He provides.

We are labelled hungry, we are labelled thirsty, we are labelled less-than, we are labelled as lame, we are labelled as worthless, yet He re-labels us with love.

Ultimately, to all people, the hungry and the physically obsessed, amidst all this messy humanity, our Jesus speaks the language of love and He gives an abundance of all we need.

His love transforms us. We are made new.

John's message, the fourth book of the New Testament, is not just a collection of fun stories.

The writer of John does not just randomly select a few of Jesus' best messages.

No. These messages shepherd us into a profound discovery: That there is no label we may put over ourselves, there is no label our culture can apply to us, there is no label we can place over anyone, there are no labels that will ever supersede the label Jesus Christ has placed over us. We are given the label of love.

We are labeled as love.

As we accept this label, we discover we are invited to grow closer to Christ. We are invited to seek to see His label lifted high over any we might ever consider.

Turn to Jesus, let His label be your label.

Will you let Him label you with His love?

I Am Who I Am

John 7 - 9 & Revelation 1:12-18

Let's play a game.

On this page, there is a list of quotes. Your task is to read each one of them, then guess who said each line.

The correct answers are on the next page.

Here are the quotes:

1. "I am not a crook."
2. "I am inevitable."
3. "I am your father."
4. "I am good, but not an angel."
5. "I am too sensitive a person"
6. "I am Ironman."
7. "I am not The Rock."

Answers:

1. Richard Nixon
2. Thanos
3. Darth Vader
4. Marilyn Monroe
5. Mike Tyson
6. Tony Stark or Ozzy Osbourne
7. "(I am Dwayne Johnson)" Dwayne Johnson

How did you do?

In the next few chapters, we are going to begin to look at some of the "I Am..." statements of Jesus. They are threaded throughout the Book of John; they help us to identify some of the ways God's Word labels the person we know as Jesus Christ.

First, let's revisit the Book of Exodus. The Exodus story provides valuable context for understanding the "I Am..." statements we will explore.

Exodus 3 recounts the story of Moses' encounter with God.

Beginning in 3:2, we read:

> [2] ... the angel of the Lord appeared to him [Moses] in flames of fire from within a bush. Moses saw that though the bush was on fire it did not burn up. [3] So Moses thought, "I will go over and see this strange sight—why the bush does not burn up."

> [4] When the Lord saw that he had gone over to look, God called to him from within the bush, "Moses! Moses!"

> And Moses said, "Here I am."

[5] "Do not come any closer," God said. "Take off your sandals, for the place where you are standing is holy ground." [6] Then he said, "I am the God of your father, the God of Abraham, the God of Isaac and the God of Jacob." At this, Moses hid his face, because he was afraid to look at God. [67]

From out of this mysterious burning bush, God calls to Moses and introduces Himself using an "I am..." statement. He says, "I am the God of your father, the God of Abraham..."

If you were to continue reading through Exodus chapter 3, you'd read how God then begins to tell Moses how He, how God, will rescue the people of Israel from their enslavement in Egypt. As part of this plan, God instructs Moses to go before Pharaoh, the king and ruler of Egypt. He is to demand that the Pharaoh set the people of God free.

Moses is, however, reluctant.

In verse 11, Moses says to God:

[11]... "Who am I that I should go to Pharaoh and bring the Israelites out of Egypt?" [68]

God tells Moses, simply, "I will be with you..." [69]

This does give Moses confidence. We can see the evidence of such affirmation in his actions. For example, as we continue reading the story, it becomes obvious that it is not the "standing-in-front-of-Pharaoh" that causes the most concern for Moses.

Rather, it is the task of representing, or speaking on behalf of God. Moses appears to fear the prospect of proclaiming God's message to the people of Israel. He fears speaking on behalf of the One True God more than he fears the Egyptian court.

Pay attention to the tension in these verses:

¹³ Moses said to God, "Suppose I go to the Israelites and say to them, 'The God of your fathers has sent me to you,' and they ask me, 'What is his name?' Then what shall I tell them?"

¹⁴ God said to Moses, "I am who I am. This is what you are to say to the Israelites: 'I am has sent me to you.'"

¹⁵ God also said to Moses, "Say to the Israelites, 'The Lord...'" [70]

Take note here, "The Lord..." is translated from the Hebrew word Yahweh. It is the proper name of the God of Israel. [71]

The God of Israel identifies Himself simply as "I am who I am." [72]

Their dialogue continues in verse 15.

¹⁵ God also said to Moses, "Say to the Israelites, 'The Lord, the God of your fathers—the God of Abraham, the God of Isaac and the God of Jacob—has sent me to you.'

"This is my name forever,

the name you shall call me

from generation to generation. [73]

Moses is then dispatched on a mission of emancipation.

Moses is sent as a representative of God's holy name, not his own.

Moses is sent to set the chosen people of God free from their bondage of slavery under the Egyptians.

It is a mission that is eventually fulfilled, in the proper time, by Jesus. Moses' obedience is a step towards God rescuing all of us from slavery. Through His plan, we are set free from the slavery of sin.

The calling of Moses in the Exodus story is significant in helping us understand Jesus' "I Am... " statements in their proper context.

In Exodus, we see God introduce Himself in the most absolute of terms.

Again, Exodus 3:14 says,

> [14] God said to Moses, "I am who I am. This is what you are to say to the Israelites: 'I am has sent me to you.' " [74]

Let Me Introduce Myself

Simply put, an "I am..." statement is a common way to introduce ourselves to others.

We say, "I am..." then we add some descriptor of ourselves.

Hello. I am Michael.

I am a Pastor.

I am Rose's husband. I am a dad. I am "Pop" to my grandson, and I am also a son. I am a son-in-law. I am an American.

I am a Marine.

I am a man.

I am a farmer.

I am a beekeeper.

I am an author.

I am a friend.

I am imperfect, but I am also a decent human being.

I am kind.

I am good.

I am fun.

I am happy.

I am loving.

We can each create various "I am..." statements about ourselves. This can lead to an oversimplification of what is happening when we read this phrase in the Bible.

God, in a demonstration of His absolute sovereignty and completeness, does not need any introduction or additional explanation of Himself.

He simply says, "I am who I am." Because God exists outside of time, this passage may also be translated as "I will be who I will be" or even "I will be what I was." [75]

Where we use these statements about the self to expand on our identity and to attach labels describing our unique or common characteristics, God does not. In essence, God says He is unchanging and outside of our ability to label or explain Him.

God, simply put, exists. He is constant and faithful.

I struggled to comprehend the profound and divine nature of this concept by attempting to contextualize it within our modern world. That's why this chapter began with the "Guess who said this..." quote game.

"I am..." is a powerful statement of individualism and identity.

It is how we seek to define our existence.

Names of God

Listen to how the *New Bible Commentary* explains God's use of "I am..."

> "Moses' request for God's name is important because the Israelites believed that the name reflected an individual's essence. In Genesis, different aspects of God's nature are highlighted by the names used to designate him: [these are names humans use to try and explain who God is]
>
> - *El Elyon* (God Most High; Gn. 14:18–20),
> - *El Roi* (God who sees me; Gn. 16:13),
> - *El Shaddai* (God Almighty; Gn. 17:1),
> - *El Olam* (the Eternal God; Gn. 21:33)." [76]

There are many more "names of God," but there is only one God.

Similar to how we introduce ourselves, we try to use labels to explain aspects of God's character in terms we all understand.

The Lexham Survey of Theology explains that "Scripture often employs metaphorical names for God in order to emphasize a certain aspect of his character or of his relationship with humanity." [77] This allows the writer to both "utilize imagery in a poetic fashion" and to help the reader relate to "God with something in the created world." [78]

The name "Yahweh" is, however, different. Unlike other monikers used to describe a characteristic of God, Yahweh simply translates to "He is what He is." [79] "Furthermore, his nature does not change" it reminds us that He is "the God worshipped by earlier generations (*the God of Abraham, the God of Isaac and the God of Jacob*) and generations yet to come (*this is my name for ever, the name by which I am to be remembered from generation to generation*)." [80]

Ideally, this adds a profound amount of clarity to what we read next from Jesus.

Understanding the profoundness of these "I am" statements is so crucial. However, it is necessary for us to see it in the proper context.

Everyone from His closest disciples, to the crowds gathered to hear Jesus speak, to the religious elite of the day would have understood Jesus was not just identifying His personal characteristics. He was equating Himself to something more.

"I Am..."

To begin to understand what Jesus is saying about His identity, we can start by considering John 8:58. Here, Jesus begins with another "Very truly" statement. He is going to make a bold statement that is indisputable.

A fact that cannot be denied. Jesus says:

> [58] "Very truly I tell you, " ... "before Abraham was born, I am!" [81]

By first referencing Abraham, the father of Judaism, Jesus is referencing the beginning of God's covenantal relationship with the people of Israel. Jesus makes it clear that He existed generations and centuries before Moses, and He proclaims Himself as pre-existing by using the same language as God, as Yahweh, as Creator, as King, and as Father. Jesus uses the same eternal language that God that God used when He proclaimed Himself to Moses.

> [58] "Very truly I tell you, " ... "before Abraham was born, I am!" [82]

Do not miss the utterly profound nature of this statement. Jesus, in each of His "I am..." statements, professes His identity as God in the flesh.

If you have studied the "I am" statements before, you'll note the confession in John 8 is not the first time Jesus has made an "I am..." statement in the Book of John.

In John chapter 4, we see Jesus using one of these statements in His label-changing dialogue with the woman at the well. This is John 4:25-26.

> 25 The woman said, "I know that Messiah" (called Christ) "is coming.
>
> When he comes, he will explain everything to us."
>
> 26 Then Jesus declared, "I, the one speaking to you—I am he." [83]

Then, in chapter six of John, Jesus equates Himself to the life-giving manna that the Jewish ancestors subsisted on in the wilderness. One such example comes from verse 47:

> 47 Very truly I tell you, the one who believes has eternal life. 48 I am the bread of life. [84]

In John 8, we witness Him continuing to assert His true identity with more "I am..." statements.

John 8:18:

> 18 I am one who testifies for myself; my other witness is the Father, who sent me." [85]

John 8:23:

"You are from below; I am from above. You are of this world; I am not of this world. [24] I told you that you would die in your sins; if you do not believe that I am he, you will indeed die in your sins." [86]

And there are many more examples of these bold statements professed by Christ.

In fact, when you are reading the Book of John, I'd encourage you to underline, or highlight, or just pause and take note of each time you see one of these "I am" statements appear.

They are incredibly important for understanding Jesus' true identity because it is how He chooses to introduce Himself to the world.

But Why?

I always love this question: "Why does it matter?"

Why should we care that Jesus said "I am..." multiple times?

Why spend so much time on who He claims Himself to be?

To be honest, it matters quite a lot.

For example, John 8:12 is one of my favorite "I am..." statements. Jesus says:

[12] ... "I am the light of the world. Whoever follows me will never walk in darkness, but will have the light of life." [87]

Casually, we might just dismiss this as Jesus proclaiming Himself to be the opposite of darkness. It is that, but understanding the earlier chapters of John's writing helps us to see a deeper meaning.

Yes, the writer of John has used the word light before. In fact, "light' is a theme throughout John's testimony about Jesus. It matters because understanding it has the power to transform and deepen our faith.

This idea of light is first presented in chapter one of John. In some ways, it parallels the Creation story from the Book of Genesis. [88]

Below, I'm going to share verses 2-5 of John. However, I'm going to expand some of the words, in brackets, to add meaning and emphasis.

> [1] In the beginning was the Word, and the Word was with God, and the Word was God.

> [2] He [Jesus Christ] was with God in the beginning. [3] Through him all things were made; without him nothing was made that has been made. [4] In him [Jesus Christ] was life, and that life was the light [and illumination of truth] of all mankind. [5] The light [of God found in Jesus Christ] shines in the [moral and spiritual] darkness, and the darkness has not overcome it. [89]

In John 3, this idea of "light" comes back into the narrative.

In John 3:16, and the following verses, we read:

> [16] For God so loved the world that he gave his one and only Son, that whoever believes in him shall not perish but have eternal life. [17] For God did not send his Son into the world to condemn the world, but to save the world through him. [18] Whoever believes in him is not condemned, but whoever does not believe stands condemned already because they have not believed in the name of God's one and only Son. [19] This is the verdict: Light has come into the world, but people loved darkness instead of light because their deeds were evil. [20] Everyone who does evil hates the light, and will not come into the light for

fear that their deeds will be exposed. ²¹ But whoever lives by the truth comes into the light, so that it may be seen plainly that what they have done has been done in the sight of God. [90]

These verses about light are not unintentional. John is trying to help us see that Jesus is light, and that light is love, which illuminates every part of the world and destroys the darkness. John is plainly communicating that the light of Creation, all the way through the teachings of Jesus to Jesus' own proclamation of being the light, is a message of love.

But wait, there's more, and this is exceptionally good.

To help illuminate this point, pun intended, let's turn to John chapter 9.

In John 9, we read the story of a man who was blind. The story of a blind man being healed is indeed a miracle. However, it is far greater than just the physical healing of bad eyesight.

To understand, let's consider John chapter 9, beginning in verse 1, and what follows.

> As he [Jesus] went along, he saw a man blind from birth. ² His disciples asked him, "Rabbi, who sinned, this man or his parents, that he was born blind?"
>
> ³ "Neither this man nor his parents sinned," said Jesus, "but this happened so that the works of God might be displayed in him. ⁴ As long as it is day, we must do the works of him who sent me. Night is coming, when no one can work. ⁵ While I am in the world, I am the light of the world." [91]

Jesus helps us to see that sometimes bad things happen simply because we live in a world filled with darkness and despair. However, we also see that Jesus is the hope of this broken world. Jesus declares this by equating Himself to the life-giving light of the Creator:

"⁵ While I am in the world, I am the light of the world." [92]

For those of you who know the story, you know that Jesus then heals the blind man in the humblest of ways.

He spits in the dirt and makes a little mud.

Then, Jesus rubs this earthen material on the dysfunctional eyes of the blind man and sends the man to wash his face in a spring within the city of Jerusalem, a place called Siloam.

The results: miraculous.

The blind man is healed of his seemingly permanent, since birth, blindness.

The blind man is literally transformed from a life of darkness and brought into the light.

John's narrative goes on to explain that some people doubted this blind person's account of the events of his healing. Yet, there he is, reporting to the religious leaders at the Temple that he has been healed. He is giving an account of having been brought miraculously into the light. The formerly blind man proclaims his identity in a powerful and bold statement.

John 9:9 recounts this moment:

⁹ ... But he himself [the formerly blind man, testifying of his own identity] insisted, "I am the man." [93]

"I am the man," he announces!

As he does, the healed man helps us see why it matters that Jesus is light. When we embrace Jesus and come into the light, healed of our former darkness, our identity is changed, and it transforms how others see us and how we see the world.

We are Light

Of course, the Pharisees are put off by the increased attention surrounding Jesus. They try to get the formerly bound-to-darkness man to testify against Jesus. But remember, Jesus had rubbed mud into the blind man's eyes and had sent him away to wash up; this man had never seen Jesus. The healed man has only experienced Jesus, and having experienced Jesus' love has brought him out of the darkness and into the light.

The healed man, with his eyes opened to the truth, confesses all he knows about Jesus to the Pharisees. He makes a bold statement to the facts and to his newfound faith, even as they try to get him to make accusations that Jesus is a sinner.

John 9:25 records for us the man's response and helps us to see the invitation we each are presented with by Jesus' "I am..." statements:

> [25] He [the blind man] replied, "Whether he [Jesus] is a sinner or not, I don't know. One thing I do know. I was blind but now I see!" [94]

Wow!

Unable to have seen Jesus, the man simply states an account of the seemingly impossible thing he has witnessed. A man who said of Himself, "I am the light," has brought a person trapped in darkness into the realm of those who can see.

What judgment could the man give against such a healing?

Apparently, he could only testify that what he experienced was an act of profound and perfect love.

Still, we might question why Jesus healed this man.

Was it for some greater purpose, or was it just to help the man feel better about himself?

I think it is to demonstrate His power over all kinds of darkness. Jesus does not just say "I am light..." without also making it clear that it is much more than a study in how well our physical eyes work.

In fact, Chapter 9 of John ends with Jesus returning to the healed man's story. As John writes about their interaction, we are invited to experience and consider it as a type of exclamation point in the narrative.

Ultimately, we see that Jesus has come to heal the world of more than just physical ailments. He has come to heal us from spiritual blindness. Jesus completes the metaphor of light, love, grace, and truth as being able to destroy darkness and all evil by teaching that we must first confess our blindness and admit we are lost in the darkness before we can come to His perfect light.

So, let's pause for a moment of confession.

A confession is simply an act of humility in which we demonstrate our guilt or shortcomings. In a spiritual sense, it is much more powerful when spoken aloud to a person we can trust for accountability. If, however, that is not an option for you, I'd urge you to spend a moment in prayer and have some time of confession with God.

The man we have just learned about in John's Gospel, the blind man who was in darkness from the moment of his birth, is me.

I am very much like the blind man.

I was also born into darkness.

Worse, I reveled in that pit of despair and selfishness.

Worse yet, even now, I sometimes struggle in my flesh and am drawn back to those dark places in my mind. There are scars there that haunt me and, like the people of Israel craving to go back to their old ways, I sometimes fall backwards.

I stumbled into the messiness from which I was saved.

I can be like a pig drawn to mud.

I can be a dog returning to its vomit.

I can be loathsome.

I am weak.

I am poor.

I am lost.

I am a mess.

Yet, despite my sometimes unclean and imperfect state, despite any of these labels of despair that may ever be attached to my identity, there is more to the story; there is much more to my story.

Because when I met Jesus, I came into the light of perfect love and hope.

My unseeing eyes and face got rubbed into the dirt.

My former identity was washed away.

My earthly despair and the curse of guilt taken from me.

All of this guilt, I confess, was taken because Jesus brought me into the light. His perfect and unending light of love. He offered to wash away my dirt and sin. Jesus stepped into my world and removed the power of darkness.

Jesus spoke into my soul and He said, "I am light."

And that means, Jesus' love has become a light living in me too.

Despite my confession of having come from the darkness, Jesus has spoken. He has taken over my darkness and healed me.

He said, "I am love..." and so, as I accept His forgiveness, I am loved.

... and ...

I am healed.

Because of Jesus:

I can see.

I can speak.

I can testify that He is good!

I can tell you there is light.

I can tell you, His light overcomes the darkness.

And, in my best moments when I am walking in the way of Jesus Christ, I can stand like every other blind person who has been brought into the darkness and proclaim a witness of the light:

I am found.

I am changed.

I am made clean.

I am reborn into the light.

"I was blind but now I see!" [95]

Therefore, I invite you and I challenge you to ask yourself: "Who am I?"

What do you say about yourself?

Are you in the light or in the darkness?

May we ever step into the light of Jesus Christ and know only Him and His healing love!

7

I Am Life

John 10 - 12

What is the meaning of life? ... this a question one can ask in numerous ways.

How should I live my life?

What do I do with my life?

What is life? This seems to be an increasingly relevant question as we race forward with the development of artificial intelligence models.

Our definition of "life" can be connected to our existence. It is behind the ultimate question: Why do we exist?

Perhaps, we seek an explanation for this messy existence and ask:

What is the purpose of life?

What is the meaning of my life, and does anything exist beyond what I can see, experience, taste, feel, and otherwise test?

These questions are as ancient as humanity itself.

And, not to wax too poetically here, they are questions we must all wrestle with on some level.

In my personal experience, the quest to understand the deeper meaning of life and my own purpose in existence led me on an adventure. I pondered what lies beyond and what I can not see myself. The lack of answers available in my own limited life pointed me to an expedition of discovery.

I tried all types of things to find an answer to the meaning of life:

- Partying
- Education
- Philosophy
- Adventure
- Religion

At each attempt, I asked a question into the void:

"Is this what life is all about?"

No answer was ever given.

None.

Nothing.

Nada.

However, that all changed when I began to have a relationship with Jesus.

In Christ, I found a singular truth that gave me a purpose in life.

God gave me a reason for existence.

God answered the questions my soul longed for.

Every question I spoke into existence, He provided an answer to.

Light of All Life

In the last chapter, we revisited John's introduction (chapter 1) to understand the concept of light as a metaphor for the truth of God being brought into our world.

We learned that light is a spiritual truth able to supersede the physical, but at the same time, physical and spiritual light work together to help define much of our existence. In this combined understanding of light, we learn that God's perfect light is both physically and spiritually impossible to escape.

If we look again into John chapter one, we see this truth deepens to give us additional layers of meaning.

For example, I'd like to draw your attention to how the writer of John begins with the creation story. Then, *just as a reminder*, we see Jesus equated with God's spoken Word. We then discover His love is the light of all that exists. John calls this "the light of all mankind." [96]

Jesus is the light of all life.

Take a moment to read, once more, how the Gospel of John begins. However, as you do, pay special attention to the use of the word "life."

This is John 1, beginning in verse 4, with emphasis added for your convenience:

> [4] In him was **life**, and that **life** was the light of all mankind. [5] The light shines in the darkness, and the darkness has not overcome it. [97]

Next up, we begin to read about the foretold prophet, John the Baptist. He was the one who was predicted by the prophets of old to come and prepare the way for Jesus.

John tells us in verse 7 that John the Baptist "... came as a witness to testify concerning that light, so that through him all might believe." [98] John was not the promised Messiah; He "was not the light." [99] He was sent to point people to the light.

John the Baptist had a purpose for his life. It was to prepare the way.

John 1:9-13 explains the Baptizer's purpose this way:

> [9] The true light that gives light to everyone was coming into the world. [10] He was in the world, and though the world **was made** through him, the world did not recognize him. [11] He came to that which was his own, but his own did not receive him. [12] Yet to all who did receive him, to those who believed in his name, he gave the right to become children of God—[13] children born not of natural descent, nor of human decision or a husband's will, but born of God. [100]

John, the Gospel writer, explains that John the Baptist and Jesus both had a purpose to their life.

The Baptist's purpose was to point people to the true light.

The light's purpose, Jesus' purpose, was to illuminate us with God's love. He was to give us "the right to become children of God." [101]

Jesus was to be the light, as we have previously discussed. However, His purpose was to be that light for all the world. His very life was a light of hope; He is the light of all life.

In the Flesh

Jesus is more than just some mythological light of hope and love. John's writings also give us assurance that Jesus lived amongst us as a physical human being. He was here, on Earth, in the flesh.

This is what it means when Christianity proclaims Jesus was both God and man.

He was and is and ever will be God in the flesh.

Of course, don't take my word for it. Let's continue to look at John 1 by examining what is written in verse 14:

> [14] The Word became **flesh** and made his dwelling among us. We have seen his glory, the glory of the one and only Son, who came from the Father, full of grace and truth.[102]

The Greek word translated to "flesh" (in verse 14) means "the physical material out of which the body is composed" or, simply put, it is our physical state of existence.[103]

Therefore, when we read verse 14, it is quite literally communicating to us that:

> [14] The Word became flesh (God became physical in bodily form) and made his dwelling among us.

The statement that follows, "We have seen his glory..." reminds us that the writer of John is making a testimonial statement about what he has witnessed.

I know for long-time believers this probably seems very elementary. Just don't miss the opportunity to reflect upon it once more. This statement of Jesus being God in the flesh is of utmost importance to our understanding of God's love. For example, it means that when we read Jesus'

"I am" statements, we are not just reading a story, we are witnessing a continuation of this same physical and eye witness evidence about God's existence and nature.

Jesus is God in the flesh.

Therefore, His proclamations about Himself give us meaning to everything.

They even provide us with an answer to the deep questions we might have about our life and the meaning of our existence.

When Jesus says in John 8:58:

> 58 "Very truly I tell you," ... "before Abraham was born, I am!"[104]

He is testifying to His own eternal nature.

John 1:10 helps to underscore the significance of this statement of pre-existence when it says:

> 10 He was in the world, and though the world was made through him, the world did not recognize him.

The point for us to take away is that the eternal, spiritual creator chose to be humbled into the temporary, physical, created form.

He who is omnipresent chose to become present. In doing so, He also became known by the created. He became known for teaching us the why of our existence.

If we extrapolate the logic in this to a deeper spiritual meaning, we can then claim each of the "I am..." statements as our own. Each proclamation is Jesus introducing Himself and making it clear who He is and why He is here.

As Jesus reveals this, He provides us with an answer to the meaning of our own lives.

It is not just "life" in general, but He provides an answer to YOUR specific purpose in life.

Each word He speaks and each miracle He performs resounds with an answer: You are loved, so be love!

The very meaning of all life is revealed in the light of Christ.

The Gate and The Shepherd

In John 10, we read another bold statement from Jesus. He declares Himself to be "the gate." He is the means by which we may approach God. Furthermore, Jesus declares Himself as the "good shepherd" who watches over all those in His flock. [105]

What does a gate and a sheep herd have to do with finding meaning for life?

Let's look at the text. In John 10:7-11, we read these words:

> "Very truly I tell you, I am the gate for the sheep. [8] All who have come before me are thieves and robbers, but the sheep have not listened to them. [9] I am the gate; whoever enters through me will be saved. They will come in and go out, and find pasture. [10] The thief comes only to steal and kill and destroy; I have come that they may have life, and have it to the full.
>
> [11] "I am the good shepherd..."

Then, a few verses later, Jesus repeats that statement again. John 10:14-15 says:

> ¹⁴ "I am the good shepherd; I know my sheep and my sheep know me—¹⁵ just as the Father knows me and I know the Father—and I lay down my life for the sheep. ... " [106]

Jesus is communicating to His followers His willingness to lay down His life for the sheep.

He is making it clear that when the enemy attacks, they will be met by the one who watches over the flock. It is important for us to understand the implications of what Jesus is saying. He will lay down His life for all. He lays down His life for you and me and all who will ever follow Him.

This word, translated into English as "life," is also an important theme throughout the Book of John.

In Greek, it is ζωή (**zōē**, *dzo-ay'*), and its definition means life. [107] It can be literal or figurative "life." It can also mean a "lifetime." It implies existence that can be either physical (in the present) or spiritual (especially in the future). [108] It is a word used to convey existence and meaning.

Jesus, in John 10:15, foretells that He will lay down His physical life for those who follow Him to experience eternal life.

Therefore, God is teaching us that the meaning of life is found only in Him. Jesus says, "I have come that they may have life, and have it to the full." [109]

Light is Life

In the next chapter of John's gospel (chapter 11), we read the story of Lazarus. In Lazarus, all of this seemingly metaphorical teaching about LIGHT and LIFE comes together in the most concrete manner..

For, just as the eternal absence of light is death, the everlasting presence of light is life.

When the writer of John writes to give witness about the healing of the blind man, it is Jesus' victory over physical life. Now, what we read about Lazarus is indicative of the same triumph over the eternal.

Chapter 11 of John tells us about how news of Lazarus' illness has reached Jesus. As He hears the news, Jesus foretells how the story will end. This helps us understand why He doesn't rush off in a hurry to heal His sick friend. To everyone watching, Jesus seems to be in no rush to leave and comfort Lazarus.

Jesus later explains to His disciples how Lazarus has "gone to sleep." In doing so, He continues to explain the eternal nature of our existence by using the ongoing metaphor of light and life.

Take, for instance, what we read in John 11:9, and following:

> ⁹ Jesus answered, "Are there not twelve hours of daylight? Anyone who walks in the daytime will not stumble, for they see by this world's light. ¹⁰ It is when a person walks at night that they stumble, for they have no light." [110]

Again, when Jesus says "light," remember He is also talking in the eternal, spiritual sense.

After these words, we read about Jesus telling His followers that "Lazarus has fallen asleep," but He will go "to wake him up." [111] You might note that the words "fallen asleep" have a sort of temporary, non-permanent tone to the dying man's condition. It implies less gravity, almost as if Lazarus has said, "Oh, don't mind me, I'm just shutting my eyes for a moment to rest."

However, as we see in the following verses, the disciples miss the point.

¹² His disciples replied, "Lord, if he sleeps, he will get better." ¹³ Jesus had been speaking of his death, but his disciples thought he meant natural sleep.

¹⁴ So then he told them plainly, "Lazarus is dead, ¹⁵ and for your sake I am glad I was not there, so that you may believe. But let us go to him."
[112]

Jesus drops the metaphor to make His point more clearly: "Lazarus is dead."

Jesus uses this moment of tragedy as a teaching point. In doing so, He connects our physical existence to a spiritual fact that He wants to explain to us.

Don't miss this, Lazarus is from our physical perspective, in permanent darkness. The man is a corpse lying at rest in a tomb. He is dead to this world.

If we allow ourselves to ponder this existence for even a moment, it forces us to pause. The status of the dead is a seemingly permanent condition. Here, amongst the living, we are invited to wonder:

- What happens when I one day die?
- Where is light when I am buried and in the darkness?
- What, then, is the meaning of our life when we are at rest from our physical existence?

I've been to many funerals, more than I can count. A person laid in a tomb is, from our limited physical perspective, a state of permanent physical darkness. To compare and contrast, it is even darker than the experience of a blind man who has been unable to see from birth.

Yet, in this moment where death seems to have conquered life, Jesus makes it clear: even the darkness of death is not permanent. As Jesus refers to the impermanent condition of His friend Lazarus as "fallen asleep," He teaches us that death is no more permanent than taking a nap. [113]

Next in the story, Jesus boldly demonstrates His victory over all darkness, even death. When He comes to the home of His friend, Lazarus, we learn that Lazarus is not only a little dead. No one there could have mistaken his condition as just asleep or taking a heavy nap. No, Lazarus is capital "D, "DEAD. He has been wrapped in burial linens, placed in a tomb, and buried away. In fact, based on the testimony of the family, the man has been dead and buried in the Earth long enough to begin to smell foul. John records for us that, when Jesus finally arrives, Lazarus had already been in the tomb for four days.

As Jesus arrives, Martha goes out to greet Him.

She is not the only one there. We also read that many Jews have come from Jerusalem to mourn with the family. The fact that others have gathered is not a random side note; it is an intentional fact. The arrival of other mourners helps people who struggle in their faith to believe; Jesus' next miracle will be performed before many eyewitnesses.

Verses 21-27 capture the exchange of words between Martha, the grieving sister of Lazarus, and Jesus:

> 21 "Lord," Martha said to Jesus, "if you had been here, my brother would not have died. 22 But I know that even now God will give you whatever you ask."

> 23 Jesus said to her, "Your brother will rise again."

> 24 Martha answered, "I know he will rise again in the resurrection at the last day."

²⁵ Jesus said to her, "I am the resurrection and the life. The one who believes in me will live, even though they die; ²⁶ and whoever lives by believing in me will never die. Do you believe this?"

²⁷ "Yes, Lord," she replied, "I believe that you are the Messiah, the Son of God, who is to come into the world." [114]

Well, let's just dig into this dialogue for a moment.

Did you catch the additional "I am... statement from Jesus in His conversation with Martha?

This is, perhaps, one of His most important "I am..." statements. It explains to us the very meaning of life.

You can test me on this. I encourage you to search and see what you can find. Search all of human knowledge and existence for a meaning to life. I believe you will never find an answer more profound than what Jesus declares here.

Jesus tells us the meaning of life can only be found in one place. It is given to us from the One who came to give us life and light.

This is profound indeed, because:

- He is the resurrection and the life.
- He is the beginning and the end.
- He is the alpha and the omega.
- He is the creator of the physical life we experience.
- He is the Lord over the eternal spiritual life we are blind to see.
- He is the shepherd who controls the gate to come into His Kingdom.
- He is the resurrection by which we move from this temporary world into the eternal, true, spiritual, and never-ending existence.

Consider again John 11:25:

[25] Jesus said..., "I am the resurrection and the life. The one who believes in me will live, even though they die; [26] and whoever lives by believing in me will never die. [115]

His statement demands our attention. It forces us to wrestle with either accepting it as truth or denying Jesus altogether. We are compelled to confront the same question that Jesus poses to Martha after His "I am..." declaration.

Jesus asks each of us:

"... Do you believe this?" [116]

He is not just asking this question of Martha. It is for each of us to decide as well.

Do you believe this?

Do you believe Jesus is "the resurrection and the life" and that by believing in Him we "will never die?" [117]

His light is life and as we lean closer into His message, we discover we must make a choice.

Why Are You Here?

We started this chapter with some open-ended questions about the meaning of life.

"What is the meaning of life?"

Based on the teachings of Jesus, I'd like you to consider the following answers. Again, these are the answers I've found. As you read these words, I encourage you to seek out these answers so you may have a sense of ownership of them for yourself.

You have to answer for yourself. My faith will not save you.

What is life?

> For me, it is Jesus.

What is the meaning of life?

> For me, it is knowing Jesus.

How should I live my life?

> For me, it is by following in the Way of Jesus.

What do I do with my life?

> I will tell others about the love of Jesus.

Jesus said for all who will listen, this bold statement of truth:

> "I am the resurrection and the life. The one who believes in me will live, even though they die; [26] and whoever lives by believing in me will never die. [118]

Then, He asks each of us:

> "... Do you believe this?" [119]

Well, do you believe this?

If so, then may we live as if it is true in every part of our existence.

Just What The Father Has Told Me

Take a moment to pause here.

Take a moment to pause and pray or simply reflect. Do you believe in Jesus Christ as your Lord and Savior?

Pause.

Take a deep breather.

Spend a moment here.

When you are ready, read these next few verses from John 12:44-50.

> [44] Then Jesus cried out, "Whoever believes in me does not believe in me only, but in the one who sent me. [45] The one who looks at me is seeing the one who sent me. [46] I have come into the world as a light, so that no one who believes in me should stay in darkness.
>
> [47] "If anyone hears my words but does not keep them, I do not judge that person. For I did not come to judge the world, but to save the world. [48] There is a judge for the one who rejects me and does not accept my words; the very words I have spoken will condemn them at the last day. [49] For I did not speak on my own, but the Father who sent me commanded me to say all that I have spoken. [50] I know that his command leads to eternal life. So whatever I say is just what the Father has told me to say."[120]

Do you believe this?

Do you believe He came to tell us just what the Father has told Him to say?

Do you believe He is who He claims to be?

If so, have the confidence in what you believe. His commands lead to eternal life. His commands are light.

Therefore, as we follow Him, let us remember to always:

- Serve one another
- Encourage one another
- Bear one another's burdens
- Love one another

It is in Christ alone that we find the meaning to our life.

He gives purpose to our existence.

He alone leads us to eternal life.

May we live as if it is true in every moment of our existence, in this life and the next.

8

I Am The Vine

John 13 - 15

Oxford Dictionary defines anxiety as "a feeling of worry, nervousness, or unease, typically about an imminent event or something with an uncertain outcome." [121]

The Mayo Clinic attempts to explain the symptoms associated with anxiety as an illness. "The causes of anxiety disorders aren't fully understood," they explain. [122] "Life experiences such as traumatic events appear to trigger anxiety disorders in people who are already prone to anxiety

and, "inherited traits also can be a factor." [123]

According to the website, WebMD, anxiety as a disorder is markedly different than normal anxiousness. They report:

> "Anxiety disorders are different from normal anxiety. They are the most common form of mental illness in the United States, affecting nearly 1 in 5 adults. They can involve periods of excessive worrying or fear that is more than you would expect from everyday kinds of stressors." [124]

Genetics, scarcity, and dependency can all cause anxiety. Meanwhile, our fears can create terrible anxiety. In my experience, understanding these challengingly tense feelings can reveal things we are connected to on an emotional or spiritual level. They can even help us uncover parts of our life that distract us from the power of God's love.

Phobias and Fears

Take for instance, some of the various fears and phobias people suffer.

Do you struggle with any of these fears or phobias?

Claustrophobia, most of us are familiar with this more common fear. It is the fear of confined spaces.

If you have **Hydrophobia**, it could be a result of rabies and may be lethal if severe. It is the fear of water.

Elurophobia is a particularly tragic phobia. Of course, that is coming from someone who admittedly loves cats. Elurophobia is the fear of cats. How sad!?

Ephebiphobia is probably far less known. If you've never heard of it, that's okay. Try and guess its meaning before you continue reading. I'll give you a hint: it is something that is far scarier than cats. It is the fear of something with bigger claws and nastier teeth. It is a menace that is much more likely to destroy your house and everything in it. Did you guess it? Ephebiphobia is the fear of teenagers. Bruh, I know this is cringe, but it feels like skibidi rizz, whatever that means, has to fit in this paragraph. It's just too bussin. No cap. [125]

Here is another one you can take a guess at: **Gamophobia**. No, it is not the fear of games. It is a fear of deep connection to one another; it literally means the fear of marriage.

Philophobia is kind of related, gamophobia. It is often the result of deep emotional scarring. If you are reading this book, a book seeking to explore the love of God, then you probably don't have this condition. Philophobia is the fear of love.

Keeping with the same relational theme, have you heard of **Philemato-phobia**? No, it is not a fear of Philemon, the third shortest New Testament book that is sandwiched between Hebrews and Titus. It is the fear of kissing.

Bibliophobia, similarly, is not the fear of the Bible. It is, however, the fear of books.

Hippopotomonstrosesquipedaliophobia is a fear that seems especially cruel and unusual. It feels like the person who coined this term must have been seeking to torture those who struggle with the anxiety this condition describes. **Hippopotomonstrosesquipedaliophobia** is the fear of long words. [126]

Hopefully, you don't struggle with any of these.

Our experience with anxiety can be healthy. Some worry and fear is normal. Those emotions work to reveal the things we truly care about.

Sometimes, they expose what we are most deeply connected to in our spirit.

Podophobia

When we study the teachings of Jesus, one of the things that becomes painfully obvious is that we can easily be controlled by the things of the world. In fact, the things we are most connected to often determine the fruit of our heart and the words of our mouth. Our earth-bound ambitions become exposed in our fear and worry. The constant desiring for more can even trigger anxiety, depression, and other chronic mental health challenges.

By contrast, longing for a relationship with God and living in such a way as one who seeks to follow Jesus unleashes something altogether different in our lives. Seeking Jesus brings us into a relationship full of joy, peace, patience, kindness, and love.

In John 13, we read about Jesus modeling this change in focus for His disciples. It is an intentional rejection of the worldly way of thinking in exchange for seeking to build God's Kingdom.

Jesus teaches while showing that He had conquered podophobia (the fear of feet). [127] The leader, teacher, king, Lord, Messiah, Christ: Jesus, took the humble role of a servant and washed the feet of His disciples.

He does this, in part, to demonstrate true servant leadership.

I like to think of it as a revolutionary overturning of the status quo. Jesus rebels against the "me-first" attitude of those in positions of power and humbly takes a knee to serve others. In doing so, Jesus models for us the true nature of sacrificial love.

Washing feet is a radical act of love.

After Jesus performs this simple act of submission, he returns to his place at the dining table and asks those present if they understand what he has done for them. Then, He says:

> 13 "You call me 'Teacher' and 'Lord,' and rightly so, for that is what I am. 14 Now that I, your Lord and Teacher, have washed your feet, you also should wash one another's feet. 15 I have set you an example that you should do as I have done for you. 16 Very truly I tell you, no servant is greater than his master, nor is a messenger greater than the one

who sent him. [17] Now that you know these things, you will be blessed if you do them.[128]

This is the nature of following Jesus. When we follow His model of love and His example of servant-leadership, we become something different. We become blessed.

Jesus says, to those of us who choose to live in His perfect way of love, that we will be blessed.

Love in Action

Now, don't miss the point of what Jesus is teaching. He is not saying foot-washing is a blessing. It is the act of serving one another that leads to blessing.

If it were just washing feet, I think we'd find that quite strange in our modern context. One year during Holy Week, we hosted a foot-washing service at the church where I serve as pastor. Several people couldn't participate because they were just weirded-out by it. A few even told me later they held back because they hadn't gotten a pedicure recently.

I get it.

There is no need to judge people for modesty or anxiety induced by our beauty-obsessed culture.

Besides, Jesus isn't saying the washing of the feet leads to the blessing. It is the willful act of submission and service, choosing to allow God to work in and through us.

It is becoming love in action.

But how do we do that in our modern context? If it is not cleaning the feet of those we love, what is it?

Essentially, I believe we receive the same blessing anytime we act out of love. When we deny our selfish desires, wants, or needs and do something for someone else. If that person normally serves us or sees us as a leader, then those acts of love become an even deeper blessing.

Practically speaking, we have lots of ways to serve one another that carry the same cultural relevance as Jesus' "washing of the feet."

Here are just a few ideas:

1. **Serve children** - Children are often overlooked and treated as less than in almost every culture. In our homes and churches, we need to be intentional by not allowing the same low standard. Choosing to serve in the children's programs at your church or local school is a way to symbolically wash the feet of both families and children.

2. **Participate in local ministry** - Most churches offer a plethora of ministry service opportunities. To practice washing the feet of those you worship with, consider making a year-long commitment to serve in a volunteer capacity in an area of need. In doing so, you leverage your God-given talents, time, and treasures to make a Kingdom impact while showing love to your church and community.

3. **Accept less** - The Biblical practice, or holy habit, of simplicity reminds us to get by with less and to practice contentment.

   ◦ We can live in simplicity by taking less food from the food line at family gatherings or church picnics. Holding back a little allows others to have more.

   ◦ Simplicity can also be practiced when we are stewarding our financial resources. We set aside resources to serve or give to others. We choose to tithe faithfully. In doing so, we sacrifice something of value to serve someone else's needs.

   ◦ In a very practical way, we can all accept less and wash the feet of others by taking small actions into consideration.

Little things like where we choose to park our vehicles can help put others first. For example, if you are in good health, park as far away from the entrance as possible when you get to church. This creates room for those facing mobility challenges, people who are running late, families with small children, and guests.

All of these suggestions require time and effort, like washing feet. They also invite us to take a moment to make a tangible difference in someone else's life. In my experience, we are blessed by the humble act of serving, the moment when we become love in action.

The Way

The thing that dies in us when we take a knee and serve someone else is more than just our pride. In those moments, we literally become the hands and feet of Jesus. We are led by something far more important than our selfish ego.

I know from studying Sociology that, in a secular context, we would refer to such acts of devotion in the context of one's religiosity. Religiosity is a term social scientists use to measure one's level of religious devotion. Those studies help to pinpoint the challenges facing the Church today. They help us to understand how many, sadly, only practice Christianity as a religion. They ascribe to the teachings of Jesus when it is convenient or when it doesn't interfere with their personal preferences.

Yet, through the eyes of the writer of the Gospel of John, we learn that following Jesus requires much more of us than nominal adherence to the faith. Christianity is more than just a set of rules to follow. It is more than just a label. Additionally, it is not just about doing the right things, nor is it exclusively concerned with avoiding the wrong things.

Being a Christian means to be Christ-like. Therefore, following Jesus, as a Christian, is something more.

It is a way of life. It is a journey of discovery that is especially concerned with a deeper understanding of grace, mercy, forgiveness, justice, and the ultimate example of perfect love.

The early church referred to the transformative life change associated with following Jesus simply as "The Way." [129]

This moniker implies commitment to a direction. It is a lifestyle that puts us in the footsteps of Jesus Himself. As we follow Him, we become completely committed to the teacher and dedicated to Him in all we say and do.

We truly become like Christ.

Part of the good news of John's gospel is that it reminds us that this path, of following Jesus, is open to everyone. It is even open to those who mess it up the worst.

For example, when Jesus foretells Judas' betrayal and Peter's denial, the decisions of each man after they have lost their way, become integral to understanding forgiveness. Grace and mercy are always available when we ask for them. This teaches us an amazing truth about The Way of Christ.

Jesus has made room for all of us!

In John 14, Jesus emphasises this point in what He says:

> [1] "Do not let your hearts be troubled. You believe in God; believe also in me. [2] My Father's house has many rooms; if that were not so, would I have told you that I am going there to prepare a place for you? [3] And if I go and prepare a place for you, I will come back and take you to be

with me that you also may be where I am. ⁴ You know the way to the place where I am going."[130]

He tells us there is room for each of us. Then, because He is addressing His followers, He assures us that we know "The Way."

A few verses later, we read another powerful "I am... " statement. Jesus says,

> ⁶ ... "I am the way and the truth and the life. No one comes to the Father except through me. ⁷ If you really know me, you will know my Father as well. From now on, you do know him and have seen him."
> [131]

It is here that Jesus also promises the Helper, the Holy Spirit—God with us. The Spirit is one of the ways God guides us closer to Him. Jesus tells us this internal way-finder, His Spirit, is available to us when we love Him and follow His Way. [132]

> ¹⁵ "If you love me, keep my commands. ¹⁶ And I will ask the Father, and he will give you another advocate to help you and be with you forever—¹⁷ the Spirit of truth. [133]

When we follow Jesus, we are equipped with His Spirit, "the Spirit of truth" to guide us in The Way. [134] As we allow His Spirit to work in us and through us, we do indeed become more Christian, more Christ-like.

But we have to choose to walk in the way of Jesus.

The Vine

If the way of Jesus is about connecting to Him, how can we best explain such a deeply rooted existence? In the first verses of John 15, Jesus provides a beautiful teaching to bring together the themes of love and light and life.

Jesus proclaims [1] "I am the true vine, and my Father is the gardener."

It is a teaching capable of bringing together so many of the things we've already learned from looking the Book of John. [135]

Take a moment to read John 15:1-17, provided below. As you do, I'd like to invite you to consider what it means to truly be connected to Jesus as our "vine."

[1] "I am the true vine, and my Father is the gardener. [2] He cuts off every branch in me that bears no fruit, while every branch that does bear fruit he prunes so that it will be even more fruitful. [3] You are already clean because of the word I have spoken to you. [4] Remain in me, as I also remain in you. No branch can bear fruit by itself; it must remain in the vine. Neither can you bear fruit unless you remain in me.

[5] "I am the vine; you are the branches. If you remain in me and I in you, you will bear much fruit; apart from me you can do nothing. [6] If you do not remain in me, you are like a branch that is thrown away and withers; such branches are picked up, thrown into the fire and burned. [7] If you remain in me and my words remain in you, ask whatever you wish, and it will be done for you. [8] This is to my Father's glory, that you bear much fruit, showing yourselves to be my disciples.

[9] "As the Father has loved me, so have I loved you. Now remain in my love. [10] If you keep my commands, you will remain in my love, just as I have kept my Father's commands and remain in his love. [11] I have told you this so that my joy may be in you and that your joy may be complete. [12] My command is this: Love each other as I have loved you. [13] Greater love has no one than this: to lay down one's life for one's friends. [14] You are my friends if you do what I command. [15] I no longer call you servants, because a servant does not know his master's business. Instead, I have called you friends, for everything that I learned from my Father I have made known to you. [16] You did not choose me, but I chose you and appointed you so that you might go and bear

fruit—fruit that will last—and so that whatever you ask in my name the Father will give you. [17] This is my command: Love each other. [136]

"I am the vine, you are the branches," says Jesus.

Any novice gardener will assure you that the nature of the vine will clearly determine the type of fruit produced. In the truest sense, this teaching brings together the themes of love, light, and life for each of us.

Visualizing, if you will, a vine producing fruit. It is a slow and intentional process. It produces fruit naturally; it is not rushed. The fruit follows the meaning given to it by the vine.

When I shared this message with my church, I pointed out how the slowness of a growing vineyard makes this parable feel disconnected from our hurried way of life. You may find this true as well.

Connected

To help understand what Jesus is teaching us here, let's use a different analogy for a moment. Consider in your imagination a lightbulb.

The lightbulb is where we see the light emitted by a lamp. We, the followers of Jesus, are the lamp. We are designed to bear the light-emitting instrument. The light coming from the lightbulb is the light of God. It is His good fruit produced through you. Now, a lamp by itself, much like each of us by ourselves, can not do anything to create light. It is nothing more than a paperweight. However, when the lamp is properly equipped, it can chase off the darkness.

How does the lamp do this?

Well, again, it is not of its own accord. The cord of the lamp represents our human effort to connect, or plug into, something that gives us meaning and purpose. When the cord is plugged into the right thing, it produces light.

This metaphor begs a question implied by Jesus' teaching about the vine:

- What are you truly plugged into?
- What are you connected to?

Some people try to find purpose by connecting with others.

They seek the approval of family, friends, or social media followers for validation and meaning. God's light doesn't come from following people; it comes from being connected to God. When we seek only the approval of others, it leaves us empty and wanting more. Like an unplugged lamp, we are dark. We are drained of life. We may even grieve without hope when we mourn. This misplaced connection with others is one of the reasons, I think, people have a fear of love, or marriage, or intimacy. When it is out of balance, it only leaves us hurt and empty.

Following others does not connect us to the light.

Some pursue wealth.

They seek material gain as a means of finding purpose. However, money does not bring us closer to God. Light does not come from our possessions. It comes from the One who provides those possessions. When we live in pursuit of wealth, we end up disconnected from the Giver of all good things. It creates in us a vacuum for peace and comfort. We become drained of contentment. We lose the simple joy of being thankful.

Following wealth does not connect us to the light.

Some attempt to connect with philosophy, wisdom, or even religion.

Imagine the lamp we considered earlier. Would you try to plug it into a manmade book to create illumination? Of course not. Light does not come from the wisdom of the world; it comes from God. Seeking fulfillment from human philosophy only opens a deep chasm in our souls. In our attempt at seeking to know more, or our efforts to seem more wise before our peers, we ultimately become hypocrites and whitewashed tombs. We become arrogant and puffed up.

Following philosophy, wisdom, and religion does not connect us to the light.

Some try to connect to themselves.

In a final act of self-preservation, in an attempt to reject Christ and admit their soul's need for God, some just close their hearts off completely. I think this is why many decide (or live as if they have decided) they themselves are the only true light. They try to create a bigger-than-life persona. They refuse to die to the self. They deny Jesus' Lordship in their hearts. Those who try to create light only from themselves, incidentally, end up committing the same sin as the original enemy of God. They fall deeply into his trap in their attempt to create their own light. In the end, when we are plugged only into ourselves, we find that we are dust. We are empty. Our vain attempts leave us feeling hollow and unfulfilled, longing for true love. Then, we become afraid of anything that may take our energy or our lives. Any danger bears anxiety. Literally, everything from cats to big words becomes a threat when all we can do is love ourselves.

Following the selfish desires of our heart does not connect us to the light.

What are you truly plugged into?

What are you connected to?

When I reflect on this question myself, I must confess that I've tried all of the things listed above and more. In some ways, I was like a fool running around and trying to plug a lamp into everything but the one thing it was designed to be connected to.

That was me before I met Jesus.

Could it be you?

Alternatively, you could make a choice. You can disconnect from everything else you're pursuing and simply connect with Jesus. You could choose to plug into the giver of light.

When we plug into Jesus, we get connected.

Connected to the One who is:

The giver of love.

The giver of life.

The giver of light.

Connected to the One who says, "I am... "

I am the way.

I am the truth.

I am the light.

I am the good shepherd.

I am the gate.

I am the resurrection and the life.

I am love.

Connected to the One who says, "I am the vine."

Connected to the One who is the giver of all love and light and life.

When we are connected to Jesus, like a lamp plugged into an electric outlet, we are illuminated. However, we are only able to be transformed in this manner when we are connected to Him.

It is in Him that we become light, love, truth, life.

He gives us light. He designed it into us.

That is the meaning of the vine and the branches.

Jesus said, [5] "I am the vine; you are the branches. If you remain in me and I in you, you will bear much fruit; apart from me you can do nothing." [137]

May we ever love one another in all we do.

May we be connected to Him.

May we choose to let His light shine brightly in us and through us!

9

I Am Here

John 16 - 17 & Revelation 22:12-15

When my son was born, it was the first time I'd ever really held a baby.

It was also the first time I'd ever witnessed a baby being born.

Childbirth is bizarre!

Honestly, as a young man, just coming to grips with the idea of being a father was overwhelming. Suddenly, I was going to be responsible for a living, breathing human.

Another weird thing about being that first pregnancy was how much my wife changed. My tiny wifey had ballooned to something, let's just say, more than small. She will admit that she looked bizarre and the changes inside of her, the fact she was carrying a tiny human in her womb, were absolutely fantastic.

Babies are just full of strangeness.

Yet, childbirth is a beautiful type of miracle to witness.

A significant part of the bizarre weirdness stems from a lack of experience, where we know something is going to happen but don't fully understand it. We receive the news, we see the signs, and we experience anticipation as we await this exciting and significant event to unfold.

Sometimes, when I reflect on each of my children being brought into this world, I'm left with wonder. I remember when Wyatt was born, he is my firstborn and my only son; I remember being so amazed by every detail.

In fact, I had been overseas serving in the Marines for much of our pregnancy. At one point, I was forced to extend my deployment. The waiting, coupled with delays, made the whole experience seem like an eternity.

When I finally got home, my wife (Rose) was very far along in the pregnancy. I had left when she had just conceived. When I stepped off the plane and hugged her, seven months later, the transformation was undeniable. She was very much with child.

Eventually, the moment finally came, and Rose said, "We need to go to the hospital... NOW."

Still, even as we were rushing into the hospital, it was hard to come to grips with what was happening. This thing we had waited for, dreamt about, and imagined happening, it was finally actually here.

The baby was coming!

We waddled down the stairs from our apartment and got into our little Ford Escort. Then, we had to drive over an hour in rush hour traffic. We were living in Southern California at the time. It was all bumper-to-bumper and chaotic, with aggressive drivers on the road. If you have ever driven Interstate 5, you know exactly what I mean. It was treacherous.

We finally got checked into the hospital in San Diego and, eventually, we got a room.

At some point, we saw a doctor. They began to care for us and check all the things delivery doctors typically check.

... then, at last... the final moment arrived. It was time to deliver the baby.

I remember being confused when we reached the final few pushes. Part of the confusion may have been from the exhaustion. It was very early in the morning, and it had definitely been a long, emotional day. I remember feeling out of place and helpless.

It's hard to explain, but it just felt like something was off.

The baby was arriving, and I felt wrong.

Then, it dawned on me. Along the way, I had empathized with Rose so much that I expected to be in pain during childbirth. Thank you, Jesus, I didn't feel a thing.

What a spectacle to witness! For those of you who have never seen a baby being delivered firsthand, let me tell you, it is insane. Nothing really prepares you for seeing a tiny human emerge from a person's body.

When Wyatt was in the final push out of the womb, the doctors had Rose hold off from the final push. His head came out. Doctors sometimes pause the baby here so they can clean its nose of the waxy plugs and gunk. My understanding is that it helps the baby to breathe as soon as possible.

Well, with Wyatt, and this was like something out of a sci-fi film, he was sunny side up. That means, instead of facing down and towards Rose's back, he was facing up and towards the ceiling. The medical term for this is "occiput posterior position (OP), or posterior position," and it oc-curs in only 5 to 8% of pregnancies. [138]

As his head emerged, and they had Rose hold off for one last push, I wit-nessed something incredible. It was like a scene from *Alien*. This mushy, pale-looking creature, with eyes dilated wide open because he had never seen the light of day, suddenly opened his eyes. I remember he seemed to twist and look around the room.

I'd love to know what he was thinking in that moment of arrival. For me, it was something I'll never forget. I got to witness that first moment, with my son opening his eyes to the world for the first time. It was so amazing!

Finally, there was a big push, and we had a baby boy.

He was here!

Make Straight The Way

When we bring a child into the world, it is a moment filled with antic-ipation and wonder. Whether or not you have had the joy of that expe-rience, we all have suffered through the longing for a moment to arrive, or perhaps for one to be over.

At some point in our lives, we deal with longing. When we desire some-thing to happen, it feels like the seconds pass too slowly.

- As children, we might experience the impatience of waiting for Christmas morning.
- When we fall in love, we often wait to "seal the deal" as we plan our futures together. Alternatively, we might long for that other person to reciprocate their interest. We long to feel loved.

- If you have ever been separated from someone due to work or military deployment, you know firsthand what it's like to wait for the moment to be reunited with your loved one.
- For those of you who have lost someone close to you, a child, parent, spouse, or dear friend, you know the painful waiting to be reunited in eternity with them. The lonely waiting to heal from grief that seems to never end.

Waiting for something to happen is a humbling part of the human experience. It reminds us of our finite existence and our inability to control all aspects of our lives.

We use words like "anticipation," "longing," or "desiring" as an attempt to explain the emotion connected to our hope for some future moment.

Our waiting for a future event invites us into celebration.

- We celebrate the moment the gift is received.
- We celebrate the awaited proposal and wedding.
- We celebrate the reunion when someone returns.
- One day, when we go home, we will celebrate our eternal reunion with God and all who have gone before us.

What a sweet day that will be; and, what a blessing to live and long for all our future hopes!

At our church, in Georgetown, Indiana, we have a tradition of celebrating Palm Sunday. I know that many churches only make a casual reference to the occasion. However, when we allow ourselves to consider the moment celebrated annually on the Sunday prior to Easter, we see a great invitation to celebrate.

Palm Sunday is a day filled with memories of the world's longing for the most important moment in all of history: the triumphant arrival of the promised Messiah.

John and the other gospel writers each retell the celebratory cheers of those gathered in Jerusalem that day. Their hopes and dreams were being unveiled before their eyes. People broke out in cheers. They laid their coats on the ground in front of Jesus. They waved palm branches in the air and shouted words of praise to God. In fulfillment of the prophecies, they even put him upon the back of a donkey. [139]

Again, it was such a powerful moment that it is mentioned in all four gospel accounts of the New Testament. [140]

The people were making way for what they had longed for. It must have been overwhelmingly joyful.

Why was there such anticipation for this foretold moment?

One reason for their longing was connected to what we read at the beginning of John's Gospel account.

If you recall, John's Gospel begins by explaining to us that Jesus is the Creator and that He has always existed. He is one with the Father. It is a profound proclamation that equates Jesus with God.

Also in John 1, we are introduced to a man known as John the Baptist. John, the writer, tells us that John the Baptizer had come "to testify concerning that light, so that through him all might believe."

When the Jewish leaders sent people to question John the Baptist about his identity, we read in John 1:23 that he:

> 23 ... replied in the words of Isaiah the prophet, "I am the voice of one calling in the wilderness, 'Make straight the way for the Lord.' "[141]

John the Baptist was proclaiming that God is coming into the world to bring light, love, and hope to all who believe in His name. John the Baptist played a crucial role in preparing the world for Jesus. He went before

Jesus to prepare people for Christ's arrival. He said, "Get ready, the moment we've been waiting for is now!"

The world, as explained by the writer of John and the proclamations of John the Baptist, was ripe with anticipation. According to many prophecies of the Old Testament, the world was waiting for light and "the glory of the one and only Son, who came from the Father, full of grace and truth." [142]

The world was pregnant with expectation. It was desiring the hope that had been foretold by John the Baptist and every other prophet that had come before Jesus. The people gathered that day in Jerusalem celebrated because they were longing for the hope that was being delivered before their eyes.

Understanding the anticipation gives a new meaning to Palm Sunday. I think it helps us understand why people reacted with such shouts of joy and praises to God. [143]

It also seems this is when the light bulb comes on for John, the Gospel writer. For example, in John 12, when John is recalling the moment of Jesus' triumphant entry into Jerusalem, I think his realization of what was happening is why we read these words in John 12:16:

> [16] At first his disciples did not understand all this. Only after Jesus was glorified did they realize that these things had been written about him and that these things had been done to him. [144]

It feels as if John, in his integrity, is saying he didn't realize all of this had been foretold until it was later revealed to him. Maybe, it was a bit like me looking back to my son's birth, and having that moment of realization that it was not about me, but about him and my wife. They were the ones who were going to feel the pains of childbirth. I was just there to behold what had been awaited.

The people broke out in praise because they had been told to make way.

Hosanna!

Another thing the writer of John wants us to see, in his eyewitness account, comes from John 12:13. Again, this moment was something all the gospel writers mentioned. John calls attention to how the people were shouting the phrase: "Hosanna!"

Hosanna comes from a Hebrew word meaning "oh save!" and it was an exclamation of praise or adoration. Imagine, in excited praise, crying out to God: "Save!"[145] It is not a plea made in despair; it was in the faithful fulfillment of what they were witnessing.

They shouted Hosanna, "Oh save!" because He who has always been faithful was continuing to be faithful!

Then, John recounts to us how the crowd praises Jesus as the "King of Israel."

It is important to keep in mind that many of those gathered to praise Jesus are the same people who have just witnessed Jesus raising Lazarus from the grave. I think this realization gives new meaning to their shouts of Hosanna, "Oh, save!"

The people are praising Jesus as He enters Jerusalem. The long-awaited, promised, and foretold Messiah of God, God in the flesh, has come. He is arriving, as foretold, humbly riding into the Holy City to wash the feet of His disciples.

However, Jesus comes to them to:

- To rule by serving.
- To lead by loving.
- To bring forth a Kingdom that will never end.

- To create a loving world for all who will believe.

This Kingdom, with an invitation for all people, is what Jesus Himself prophesied about in John 16.

Here I Am

In Chapter 16 of John, Jesus speaks to His disciples as they sit down for one of their final moments together. He promises them the help that will always be available, saying:

> "13 But when he, the Spirit of truth, comes, he will guide you into all the truth. He will not speak on his own; he will speak only what he hears, and he will tell you what is yet to come." [146]

Jesus promises the Holy Spirit. Then, Jesus predicts His own death and resurrection.

In this moment, we see how God foretells the coming Messiah through His covenantal promise with Abraham. It is revealed that God has foretold the circumstances and details of the Promised One of God through the prophets of Old.

In every prophetic instance, Jesus delivers.

He shows up and fulfills those promises.

It is as if each prophecy points to Jesus and says, "Look, here He is!"

John 16 is chock-full of Jesus prophesying what will happen concerning His death, resurrection, and the persecution that His followers will face.

Here's the point in these predictions: Jesus gets an A+ at predicting the future.

"Here I am," He says with His words and His actions.

Do you see the pattern here?

The things we wait for most, our future hope of redemption, our release from pain and suffering, and our desire to be made right with God in every way, all lead us to the same place. All of the things we put our eternal hope in were promised ahead of time by God.

Again, in every circumstance, Jesus Christ delivers. He is always faithful.

I want you to wrestle with this question: What do you imagine the God who is faithful in all He has ever said will do when He also tells us, through the final book of prophecy, how everything will be at the end?

If He has always fulfilled every Word spoken about Himself, I think we are safe to assume He will do exactly as He says. This is a verse I often return to, found in Revelation 22:12-15, where Jesus speaks prophetically in a vision of the future. In it, He tells us exactly what to expect, this is *What to Expect When You're Expecting* from a spiritual perspective:

> [12] "Look, I am coming soon! My reward is with me, and I will give to each person according to what they have done. [13] I am the Alpha and the Omega, the First and the Last, the Beginning and the End.

> [14] "Blessed are those who wash their robes, that they may have the right to the tree of life and may go through the gates into the city. [and then He warns us]. [15] Outside are the dogs, those who practice magic arts, the sexually immoral, the murderers, the idolaters and everyone who loves and practices falsehood. [147]

Look.

His track record is perfect.

He is always faithful.

He does what He says He will do.

He says, the world is pregnant with expectation of His returning.

The signs are right there. We have never experienced it. So, like the disciples in Jesus' presence, missing the obvious, and like someone experiencing something for the first time, not knowing what to think of it all, we are left waiting. We anticipate, without fully knowing what to expect, His imminent return.

We wait, but not without hope. His word is unfolding all around us in His glory!

We must be ready.

Will you be ready?

Will you be amongst those waving palm branches and shouting: "Hosanna, Hosanna... Save, Save!" ... or will you be cowering in fear?

Will you be ready when Jesus fulfills His words and appears, saying, "I am here."

10

I Am Yours

John 18 - 20

S omewhere between the Last Supper and His arrest, Jesus prays to be glorified.

On the Thursday prior to Easter, a day we call Maundy Thursday, I like to revisit this prayer. It reminds me of what we celebrate when we come together for Communion and when we worship each week at our local church.

For context, in the moments prior to this prayer, Jesus has just promised the Holy Spirit to His followers. He has also predicted His own death.

Jesus knows what is going to happen to Him.

Jesus knows it will break the hearts of His followers.

Jesus knows it is troubling to them greatly.

Yet, He also knows it is necessary and, importantly, He continues to remind us to think eternally. He urges us not to be stuck in the rut of only thinking about the things of this present world.

When we realize what has preceded His prayer, I think it gives special meaning to what Jesus also says in John 16:33:

> [33] "I have told you these things, so that in me you may have peace. In this world you will have trouble. But take heart! I have overcome the world." [148]

Jesus is offering peace in the face of affliction and hurt.

Jesus reminds us that this world is filled with challenges and trouble.

Jesus encourages us that He has overcome the world, and we, therefore, are eternal with Him!

Then, He prays one of the most beautifully recorded prayers in all of the Bible. In fact, many churches recite and memorize "The Lord's Prayer," but that is actually "The Lord's Model Prayer." [149] It is Jesus teaching us how to pray.

In John 17, we read an incredible recording of Jesus' prayer to be glorified. It is significant because Jesus prays for His ability to fulfill the many things foretold about Him. His prayer is on behalf of all who will be saved as a result of His sacrifice.

Like the rest of John's account, it has the gravity of having been passed down to us by an eyewitness. In John 17, we read Jesus' prayer.

Take Heart

Jesus tells His disciples to "Take heart! I have overcome the world," and then He looks to heaven and begins to pray, addressing God as "Father." [150]

> [1] "Father, the hour has come. Glorify your Son, that your Son may glorify you. [2] For you granted him authority over all people that he

might give eternal life to all those you have given him. ³ Now this is eternal life: that they know you, the only true God, and Jesus Christ, whom you have sent. ⁴ I have brought you glory on earth by finishing the work you gave me to do. ⁵ And now, Father, glorify me in your presence with the glory I had with you before the world began. [151]

Jesus begins His prayer with a personal affirmation and a reminder: He knows who He is and what He is about to do. He exists to bring glory to the Father so that verse 3 may be fulfilled:

³ Now this is eternal life: that they know you, the only true God, and Jesus Christ, whom you have sent. [152]

Jesus' prayer is, therefore, for us. It is a petition to God the Father on our behalf. He understands all that hinges on His ability to complete the very purpose of His earthen presence.

His prayer, according to *Lexham's Theological Wordbook,* uses a sense of the word for "glorify" that "captures how a person's deeds or entire life can 'glorify' God when carried out with love in obedience to the will of God." Therefore, Jesus is praying for His "actions, in themselves," to bring glory to God as "they are guided by his will and carried out in order to please him." [153]

Having prayed, Jesus turns His prayers outward to His disciples.

John 17:6 continues:

⁶ "I have revealed you to those whom you gave me out of the world. They were yours; you gave them to me and they have obeyed your word. ⁷ Now they know that everything you have given me comes from you. ⁸ For I gave them the words you gave me and they accepted them. They knew with certainty that I came from you, and they believed that you sent me. ⁹ I pray for them. I am not praying for the world, but for those you have given me, for they are yours. ¹⁰ All I have

is yours, and all you have is mine. And glory has come to me through them. [11] I will remain in the world no longer, but they are still in the world, and I am coming to you. Holy Father, protect them by the power of your name, the name you gave me, so that they may be one as we are one. [12] While I was with them, I protected them and kept them safe by that name you gave me. None has been lost except the one doomed to destruction so that Scripture would be fulfilled.

[13] "I am coming to you now, but I say these things while I am still in the world, so that they may have the full measure of my joy within them. [14] I have given them your word and the world has hated them, for they are not of the world any more than I am of the world. [15] My prayer is not that you take them out of the world but that you protect them from the evil one. [16] They are not of the world, even as I am not of it. [17] Sanctify them by the truth; your word is truth. [18] As you sent me into the world, I have sent them into the world. [19] For them I sanctify myself, that they too may be truly sanctified. [154]

The final part of what we read is particularly important.

In verse 16, Jesus prays and says, "They, [His followers] are not of this world." [155]

Then, in verse. 17 Jesus asks God to sanctify His disciples. It is a word that means saved or redeemed. He asks that we be sanctified by the truth. Then, He declares in His prayer, "Your word is truth." [156]

It is worth noting the Greek word used for "word" by the writer of John. It is *logos*. This is the same word used at the beginning of John's Gospel when John explains to us that Jesus is God. [157]

For context, because that was several chapters ago, let's flip back to John 1.

Here is chapter one, verse one:

¹ In the beginning was the Word, and the Word was with God, and the Word was God. ² He was with God in the beginning.[158]

Then, in John 1:14, just a few verses later, we read this bold proclamation that connects the two as one:

¹⁴ The Word became flesh and made his dwelling among us. We have seen his glory, the glory of the one and only Son, who came from the Father, full of grace and truth.[159]

What we need to remember from John 1 is that Jesus is the Word and the Word was God, that Word became flesh in the person of Jesus Christ. He came to us, "from the Father, full of grace and truth."[160]

This adds a lot of context to John 17:17, where it says, again:

¹⁷ Sanctify them by the truth; your word is truth.[161]

Reading all of this together helps us connect the dots in John's Gospel to gain a more complete understanding of Jesus' full ministry and His message of love. Reading it with the seriousness with which it was crafted helps us to truly "Take heart" as Jesus encourages us to do.[162]

For You

Let's bring all of this together in a summarization of what John has written.

The word is our source for the truth. It reveals to us the ministry of love that came from God in the flesh, that is, Jesus Christ.

He is the Word.

The Word is God.

God has always existed.

God, the Word, became flesh and revealed to us grace and truth.

We, therefore, are sanctified, redeemed, saved through His Word.

We are made right through the Word because it is the grace, the truth, and the love of Jesus Christ.

This is the message of Jesus. It is good news for all mankind. It is the gospel.

It is also one of the many reasons we are wise to take the Book of John, John's account of Jesus' life and teachings, so seriously. It is powerful.

It is also personal.

It is for you.

On the eve of His sacrifice, Jesus prays for His disciples, for the ones who are gathered with Him in that moment. Then, perhaps as He looks out across all of the expanse of time and human history, He prays for me and you and all who will ever choose to follow Him. He prays they would be sanctified, saved, and redeemed by the truth. As He does, He again equates the word with truth.

The bottom line in our examination of His prayer from John 17 is that the word of truth saves us. The word of Jesus. The word of God.

Understanding this is a profound spiritual reality.

When Jesus prays for all believers, for you, this is what He says:

> [20] "My prayer is not for them alone. I pray also for those who will believe in me through their message, [21] that all of them may be one, Father, just as you are in me and I am in you. May they also be in us so that the world may believe that you have sent me. [22] I have given them the glory that you gave me, that they may be one as we are one—[23] I in

them and you in me—so that they may be brought to complete unity. Then the world will know that you sent me and have loved them even as you have loved me. [163]

Jesus reveals that He is giving the disciples, including you and me, gifts to help us remain in unity. It is not for unity's sake alone. In our ability to stand together, the world will know, according to Jesus' prayer:

"... that you [God the Father] sent me and have loved them even as you have loved me."

Finally, Jesus prays:

24 "Father, I want those you have given me to be with me where I am, and to see my glory, the glory you have given me because you loved me before the creation of the world.

25 "Righteous Father, though the world does not know you, I know you, and they know that you have sent me. 26 I have made you known to them, and will continue to make you known in order that the love you have for me may be in them and that I myself may be in them." [164]

Jesus' prayer concludes with this hope-giving request. His heart's desire is for us to know Him and to experience the love of God the Father through His model of love and His teaching.

What I urge you to understand is that this prayer of Jesus is for us today.

It is His intent, His purpose, His heartfelt desire that we would be in unity with Him.

He yearns for us to be one with God through the Holy Spirit.

May we never forget the new commandment He has given us:

[34] "A new command I give you: Love one another. As I have loved you, so you must love one another. [35] By this everyone will know that you are my disciples, if you love one another." [165]

Jesus proclaims to us, in His prayer, that He is ours.

When we follow Him, we too are His.

I Am Love

John 20 & John 15

Sometimes, when I am writing or rewriting my sermons, as I have for this book, I pause and wonder why I put so much work into them. More than once, I've tried to explain my efforts to my family or friends. I've spent time justifying how I spend my time to my Elders at church.

At the end of the day, it comes down to calling.

As one called to follow Jesus, my hope is to invite others to grow in their knowledge and understanding of how He has brought purpose to my life. As a pastor, I want to see my church become restored into the completeness of God's love. As a husband, father, and "pop," I stretch myself to practice what I preach. As I pursue each of these things, those around me will be blessed. Not only will I leave my family with an example of someone transformed by God's perfect love, but I will also get the blessing of living out love with all the people in my life.

This book, the one you are reading, *God Called Love*, originated in a study through the Book of John. It was a sermon series called "I Am. Love," and it was created to focus on challenging us to be love in action. In my experience, when we study John's eyewitness account of the life and ministry of Jesus Christ, it opens our hearts and minds to grow in our faith truly.

It is impossible to consider John's account and not be changed.

Part of that transformation comes from being firmly connected to Jesus Himself. As mentioned in an earlier chapter, Jesus is our vine, and we, when we are connected to Him, are an extension of all He is.

He is love.

When we are rooted in Him, we too become love.

If we were to boil this down and simplify it, we could not do so without remembering what Jesus says in John 15:17:

> 17 This is my command: Love each other.[166]

We may try to follow any number of ways of thinking in this world. When we do, we become connected to those things instead of Jesus. The fruit of those vines is apparent in the brokenness of lives left in despair, devoid of true love.

Anything we try to draw strength from will ultimately lead to more fear and anxiety.

In the most profound, most spiritual sense, we must strip away all the trappings that surround us and embrace only Jesus. He is how we are tethered to God.

He is love.

In Him, we too become love.

Easter

Often, when I read the Bible to prepare my sermons or edit my writings, I like to try to put myself in the shoes of those I'm reading about. For one, it helps to bring the text to life. Secondly, it gives me insights into what is written that I might have otherwise missed. Additionally, immersing myself in the story helps me extract the truth instead of just looking for confirmation of what I already believe.

This is no small task.

For example, if we consider the moment we celebrate each Easter from the perspective of those who were there, it brings it to life. We may imagine ourselves as the disciples witnessing Jesus' crucifixion. In our mind's eye, we could imagine being one of the women who came first to the empty tomb. There seems to be no end to the imaginative ways we can place ourselves into the story through John's eyewitness account.

If we were to consider the perspective of those who were present at the foot of that torturous cross, what questions might we have asked?

Would we have wondered:

What happens when Jesus is gone?

When He is taken away, where do we go, who do we follow?

When He is put to death and buried, is that the end?

The answers to those questions help to shed light on what we celebrate at Easter. They also bring light into the darkness of the empty tomb. They even illuminate the places where fear, anxiety, and worry take refuge in our hearts.

One of the most incredible and powerful points of our annual celebration of Easter is this: God was present. He walked amongst us.

Then, in the most horrible of ways, He was taken away. Jesus was put to death by those selfishly opposed to His radical message of love.

When we put ourselves into that moment, we can see Him there: hanging on the cross, drained of life.

Christ was dead.

He was wrapped in burial clothes.

They placed His body in a tomb.

The stone was rolled shut and sealed.

In that moment, would it not seem as if love itself had been laid to rest?

However, what seemed like the end of the story was, in fact, just the beginning.

He defeated death and came out of the tomb. It is the very moment we celebrate every Easter.

Witness to Love

Not everyone is good at imagination. It is one of the things that makes history boring to some and exciting to others: the ability to imagine ourselves in those past moments.

Well, let's lean into the imagining for a bit. I'll do my best to be your tour guide and to paint a picture from the perspective of those we read about in John's account of Jesus' death.

We can consider John's testimony to see how Jesus' closest followers responded to the moment they were disconnected from Jesus through His death. As we do, I think we see in them several options for what we also might do when we find ourselves feeling far from God.

Mary Magdalene - This is not Mary, the mother of Jesus. Mary was the first to witness the empty tomb of Jesus. Her account is recorded at the beginning of John 20.

Well, who is this Mary Magdalene?

What we know about her is that she is a woman whom Jesus healed. In Luke 8, we learn she had been healed of seven demons. [167] If we place ourselves into the shoes of someone who would have experienced a miraculous healing, then we can easily see how Mary would be incredibly and faithfully devoted to Jesus. In Him, she would have found forgiveness, purpose, life, light, and undeniable love.

Mary Magdalene, likely due to her devotion, is a significant follower of Jesus. Not that it is a competition, but she is mentioned in the gospel accounts more frequently than many of the other male disciples.

To gain some understanding of Mary Magdalene's character, we can consider Luke's account of her life after Jesus healed her. This is from Luke 8:1-3:

> [1]... Jesus traveled about from one town and village to another, proclaiming the good news of the kingdom of God. The Twelve were with him, [2] and also some women who had been cured of evil spirits and diseases: Mary (called Magdalene) from whom seven demons had come out; [3] Joanna the wife of Chuza, the manager of Herod's household; Susanna; and many others. These women were helping to support them out of their own means.

Mary, as is clear from Luke's account, had a huge heart for Jesus. She was completely devoted to Him and followed Him, along with some other healed women, to provide support for the work of His ministry.

Perhaps her sincere desire to be close to Jesus is why He first appeared to her? We don't really know. Yet, we can imagine the impact it would have had on her.

When we place ourselves into the story from the perspective of Mary Magdalene, someone who has been healed and has a giant heart for Jesus, it brings to life the power of His teachings.

Mary had a huge capacity for faith and was powerfully devoted to God. As someone who served Jesus and helped Him out of her own means, we can learn from her witness what it means to allow His love to transform us into a new creation.

From her point of view, coming to the empty tomb must have been shocking. Matthew and Mark, in their account of this moment, tell us that Mary, the Mother of Jesus, was also there.

Through the eyes of these women, we see God's glory proclaimed to people who would have been seen as less than in their culture. The formerly demon-possessed woman and the widow whose eldest son had just been crucified as a criminal became the first evangelists of the Good News.

Their witness to His love reminds us that God's message is for all people.

Peter & John - The next two people who show up at the empty tomb are Peter and John. John's account reveals a few things about their relationship and their perspective. They literally have a foot race to the tomb.

In Peter and John's running, their competitive spirit is revealed, but it also screams of their devotion to Jesus. They are excited, and urgency fills their movement.

I like to imagine this moment from John's point of view. We can envision John telling this story and laughing about how slow the older Peter was. The foot race is a deeply personal detail that John adds to his account.

Alternatively, we could imagine Peter trying to keep pace and falling behind. Either way you imagine it, John's perspective reveals something of their competitiveness with one another. It also exposes something about men in general. It opens our eyes to the competitive nature of many who desire to be first amongst their peers.

I wonder if John did not include this detail to help us take note of the way people are often tempted to compare themselves to one another. Men and women both often jockey to be number one. Because the world tends to trample on the rights of women, I wonder if that is why Jesus first appeared to Mary Magdalene, a humble woman who had been neglected and overlooked. She had no desire to put herself first.

Men and women can both fall into the trap of pride. Pride, at its root, is competitive. It seeks to create a comparison of ourselves to one another. It leads to unhealthy competition and sometimes tears down our self-image disastrously.

A good friend of mine, Brad, often used to quip, "When we compare, we lose." He's right. When we measure ourselves against one another, we lose unity. It threatens our peace. Ultimately, we lose love in our desire to be first.

Through Peter and John, we witness both the excitement of running to Jesus. However, we also see this fun caution for anyone tempted to think too highly of themselves. Besides, even with their running to the tomb, Mary would still be able to witness that neither of them was the first to arrive.

Thomas - Finally, a third person we read about is Thomas. Thomas is famously known as a doubter.

When I put myself into his shoes, I can relate to him. Because of his skepticism, I consider him more of a practical person. Maybe he was more logical in his thinking than the others? He could have been blessed with a better intellect, or he was just brave enough to say what everyone else was thinking?

Even if he was just a skeptical person, through his eyes we see a witness that is incredibly realistic. Let's be honest, what Thomas was being asked to believe is hard for anyone to grasp.

Many of us, much like Thomas, have a hard time believing Jesus is risen.

However, through the eyes of this doubter, we too are invited to also place our hands into the nail-scarred hands and spear-pierced side of Christ. We are invited to witness that Jesus had truly conquered death.

Risen for Love

Skeptics and people who struggle in their faith can approach Jesus like Thomas. They may wander from one source to the next, looking for "the right fit." They seek justification for their doubt by finding affirmation in their biases. To the skeptic, the excitement of affirming their position as unique or special often has more appeal than just accepting God at His word.

We can see this in Thomas's doubtful approach to the risen Messiah.

In the others, we see an acceptance and excitement that stems from having already overcome their doubts. Their response may differ from Thomas's due to what they have already experienced and, in some cases, witnessed. It could also be due to personality differences.

Either way, the same fact remains: Jesus was risen for love.

His love for us brought Him here, took Him to the cross, and released Him from the tomb.

That's the joy of Easter, but the story doesn't stop there.

In John 20, Jesus appears to His disciples and He calms them by saying, "Peace be with you!" He goes on to tell them:

> 21 ... As the Father has sent me, I am sending you." 22 And with that he breathed on them and said, "Receive the Holy Spirit. [169]

Jesus gives a special, advanced, pre-Pentecost pouring out of the Holy Spirit to the apostles. Some believe this is what equips them to perform the miracles we read about in Acts; others think it is just a partial outpouring to help heal their broken hearts until the day of Pentecost. [170]

Regardless, Jesus breathing upon them recalls the creation of Adam in the book of Genesis. It symbolizes a new creation and a new beginning. [171] It is the start of something new.

Jesus' breath, the breath of God, fills those who believe in Him.

The special apostolic nature of this moment is then emphasized by verse 23. Jesus says to those with Him (again, not for all believers, it is those present):

> 23 If you forgive anyone's sins, their sins are forgiven; if you do not forgive them, they are not forgiven." [172]

Jesus is giving the apostles a special blessing and privilege. John 20:23 is not intended to empower all believers to judge one another's sins. Instead, it is a reminder: God commands that power as He chooses.

This distinction is important. Sometimes we overlook this moment or apply it poorly. The apostles are being blessed by Jesus so that they may continue the work He has ordained for them.

Of course, this moment has implications for us too. Jesus is not risen, then gone forever. His arrival was not for the judgment of the world, and then, "Poof," He was gone. No, instead, He is preparing His followers to be His messengers of love.

Later, He extends the gift of the Holy Spirit to all.

It is not meant to be a gift we hide or horde.

It is for Love.

Love is offered to all.

Love across all time.

Love from God.

This love is the very reason why Jesus was risen. It is why John 3:16 is so important and cherished.

John 3:16 reminds us:

> 16 For God so loved the world that he gave his one and only Son, that whoever believes in him shall not perish but have eternal life. [173]

If we continue reading, it is made clear that this love was not for judgment. It was for salvation. John 3:17 adds so much context, even if it is often overlooked:

> 17 For God did not send his Son into the world to condemn the world, but to save the world through him. [174]

The writer of John's Gospel then uses an analogy of light to emphasize the unique spiritual truth found only in God.[175] In a modern context, we can revisit our earlier analogy of a lamp being plugged into the proper power source. Jesus shifts the power source from external to internal.

Through Jesus, we are no longer tethered to the church building or to an organized sacrificial system of ancient times.

We are directly linked to Him!

This is, of course, not to suggest there is no value in being also connected to the Church. In fact, we benefit greatly from sharing in God's Spirit with one another. It is how we grow and mature in His love.

Jesus was risen so that we would have love, and this love does not grow in a vacuum. It is meant for us to share. Through Jesus, through the Holy Spirit, we become connected to His love in us. It is a love that shines through us, especially when we share it with one another.

He Is Love

At home, we have a portable speaker that we use in various parts of the house or when we're outdoors. It is a Bluetooth device and connects remotely to, for example, our phones.

Through that little speaker, we play music that brings us joy and transforms the environment. Sometimes the music is somber, and other times it is light or poppy.

What is interesting about the speaker is how it makes no real noise of its own accord. It is transformed by whatever signals we send it into either a band, an orchestra, or even an oration. It is versatile but dependent on receiving a signal.

We, as followers of Jesus, are much like that Bluetooth speaker. When we allow His Spirit to direct us, it transforms the motivations, our essence, and everything that flows from our mouths and actions. If we allow ourselves to be connected to Jesus, He gives us the right words for the proper moment. He lives in us and through us.

There is also a battery inside the speaker we use. If the battery gets low, the power indicating light will start blinking. It is a type of warning sign. It alerts the user that the battery is almost depleted. The light communicates a need to be recharged.

If we are honest with ourselves, we live in a world filled with challenges. The daily dilemmas we face are draining.

At some point, the exertion of energy pulls us down. It drains us.

Many of us ignore the warning signs and just carry on. Like a person ignoring the "check engine" lights in their vehicle, we test fate by pushing through. We just keep going until we are drained, hoping nothing cataclysmic will happen..

Then, one day, the engine gives out. We crash in the darkness and despair. In those desperate moments, we begin to ask:

Where is hope?

Why am I so lonely?

Some of us might even start pointing the blame at God. We may give in to the temptation to think He has abandoned us. We may feel this way even when, all along, He was there. He was reaching out to us, but we were running from Him. We were refusing to connect to the giver of hope and light and life and love.

When we neglect to connect, when we refuse love, and when we run around hoping the wrong things will somehow recharge our battery, we miss the point of following Jesus. Eventually, we may even lose the ability to share His light and love.

You see, we really can't share with others what we don't first have for ourselves.

This is why studying God's Word is so important.

It is why our fellowship in a local faith community is so critical for growing in the way of Jesus.

It is why being connected to a church that teaches God's Word is essential.

When we are plugged into Jesus, we are filled with His love. We are reminded of His goodness. We are rededicated and requipped to go out into the world and share His love with all.

The exciting thing about this relationship is how it is never-ending. The more we get to know Him, the more we realize His way is so much better than our own way. He changes us from the inside out. As He does, His Spirit reverberating within us, transforms those around us. Like a speaker filling the room with beautiful music, we become an agent of change.

Jesus was risen from the grave for this very purpose: that we would be changed by His love.

It was not so that we could feel good about ourselves and pretend we have it all together on our own.

He is love.

The grace and truth of Jesus Christ, the light of God's perfect love, it is shared with all who will choose to believe. It is given to all who accept Him as their Lord and Savior.

To each who does choose to follow Him, He gives us the power to carry His light into the darkness of this world. It is a message of love that we carry, even as we are transformed into something new ourselves. We are changed as we begin rejecting our nature, the flesh, and the selfish part of ourselves. Even our capacity for potential good or bad is made new through Jesus.

We are made new until all of it is left behind, and we are remade to be made whole in Him.

We are made whole internally.

Then, we are made complete eternally.

His love is revealed in our love for one another.

His love is forever.

He is love.

When we begin to allow His love to be ours, we too become His witnesses to the world.

12

Follow Me

John 21:1-14 & Mark 1:14-20

W hat are we to do with a God who is proclaimed as love?

In 1 John 4:15-16, we read:

¹⁵ If anyone acknowledges that Jesus is the Son of God, God lives in them and they in God. ¹⁶ And so we know and rely on the love God has for us.

God is love. Whoever lives in love lives in God, and God in them. [176]

John writes, "God is love," and urges us to follow in that love. [177]

How do we reconcile our experiences in a broken world, in light of His perfect love?

Is it even possible for us to grasp the transformative power of a universal invitation to forgiving love?

If God is love and He invites us to be love, it requires us to change. How do we change?

In John's Gospel message, we learn much about the love of God. John equates Jesus with God's Word. With exceptional boldness, he helps us to understand that Jesus was not only a man, but He was God in the flesh.

God's message of love, as declared by John, therefore requires us to make a decision:

- What will we do with the invitation to follow Jesus Christ?
- Will we continue in our own way, following the world?
- Will we leave the world behind and follow in the Way of Jesus?

The key to becoming love in action, to embracing God's love entirely, is found in the answer to these questions. To be changed by God's love, we must allow His love to change us. We must open the door and allow Jesus to change us from the inside out. Once we do, we begin to follow after Him. This is how we grow: we follow Jesus.

Following Peter

At the beginning of the final chapter of John's Gospel, we read about Jesus' appearance to His disciples once more. It is after the resurrection.

Simon Peter, one of the twelve original disciples, tells John and a handful of the other disciples, "I'm going out to fish." [178] They decide to join Peter on his fishing trip. They fish all night; however, they catch nothing.

Peter has taken the lead by initiating this fishing trip. We get the sense that, since many of them were fishermen before following Jesus, it is a path leading them back to their old ways. It is the old familiar life instead of the new way of Jesus.

The reason for this turning back to the old is not made clear. Perhaps they are still in despair from witnessing Jesus' death. We can imagine that, as they are mourning and struggling with the loss of Jesus, they must be depressed. It may be a result of brokenness from seeing their expectations dashed. They had hoped and expected the Messiah to create an earthly kingdom. By now in the story, it was clear they were mistaken.

Understandably, they flounder.

For those of us familiar with depression, we know this same path. When the anxieties resume and worry seems to darken our minds, we often fall back into fleshly comforts. We step into self-centered traps, familiar habits, and even into addiction. Depression tempts us to look backward instead of forward. It unleashes crippling despair.

As someone who has wrestled with depression, I sense this could be what is happening with the disciples. John is silent on why they decided to go fishing. We are left wondering. We can't fully understand why these men, who have been following Jesus, have now returned to their past life of fishing. We can only wonder at the cause of the disconnect they are experiencing between their mission from Jesus and their actions.

Regardless, an important distinction we should not miss here is this: Peter is taking the lead. He is the one inviting them back to their old, familiar ways.

Peter's actions suggest he, maybe more than anyone else, is despairing. We get the sense Peter is still unsure of how to move forward.

Peter is a leader among the disciples. As the leader goes, so the sheep follow. Peter pulls the others down with him.

After a night without catching anything, the sun begins to rise. They see a person on the shore but do not recognize who they are. This stranger calls out to them, calling them "Friends," and asks about their catch. [179]

They call back to the figure on the shore and report that they have caught nothing.

Now, some would say, "A bad day fishing is still better than a good day working." This jest doesn't fully consider the despair these men are facing. If we focus our attention here only on the act of going fishing, we miss the important point being communicated about their actions. We miss the motivation.

For these men, fishing is not merely a hobby as it is for most of us who occasionally go fishing with a rod and reel. They have not taken a day off work for a little catch and release. They are not going out to fish for leisure.

No, they are fishing as a profession. They have chosen to try their hand at the old familiar path of their life prior to following Jesus.

Fishing is not just a sport; it is their traditional way of living. It is a means of provision. It is how they provide for themselves and their family.

As they struggle to move forward, they are going back to this comfortable routine instead of moving forward with Jesus' often uncomfortable and challenging commands of self-sacrifice.

The fishing clearly doesn't go well. Their nets are empty, and they are not having any success.

In this emptiness, we are reminded that the old way is a path to death.

Despairing, the men talk to the man on the shore. To the inquisitive stranger, they confess to having caught nothing.

Don't miss what their failure to make a catch means:

• No fish means no food.

- No food means no hope.
- No hope means no life.

Luke's Perspective

We gain additional insight into what happens next by including Luke's account of this moment. Luke records this moment with the stranger on the shore with additional details.

For context, consider Luke 5:1-11. In this passage, we read from Luke's account of Jesus calling the disciples. It is at the beginning of His public ministry, about three years earlier in the timeline from the all-night fish-a-thon we read about in John 21.

> [1] One day as Jesus was standing by the Lake of Gennesaret, the people were crowding around him and listening to the word of God. [2] He saw at the water's edge two boats, left there by the fishermen, who were washing their nets. [3] He got into one of the boats, the one belonging to Simon... [180]

For clarity, this "Simon," owner of the boat, is the Apostle Peter we have been discussing from John's Gospel. When Jesus is first calling Simon, it is before Peter's good confession. A moment that prompts Jesus to change Simon's name to Peter. This is worth noting here for clarification and also because, as we will soon see, it reminds us of who Peter was before Jesus.

Luke 5 continues and explains the calling of Simon (Peter) by Jesus. Jesus gets into Simon Peter's boat and instructs him to move a little farther out from the shore. Jesus then uses the boat as a platform to teach those standing along the coast. [181]

Next, we read:

⁴ When he [Jesus] had finished speaking, he said to Simon, "Put out into deep water, and let down the nets for a catch."

⁵ Simon answered, "Master, we've worked hard all night and haven't caught anything. But because you say so, I will let down the nets." [182]

Simon Peter is an experienced fisherman. He knows when to call it quits. Yet, he is obviously impressed with Jesus. He obeys, positions the boat, and drops the nets into the deep waters.

Suddenly, the fishermen begin to catch what Luke describes as "a large number of fish." [183] It is so many fish that they must call out to an additional boat for help. Even then, with the help of another boat, the catch is so plentiful "that they began to sink." [184]

The next few verses record Peter's response and help us to connect John, the author of the Book of John, to this moment:

⁸ When Simon Peter saw this, he fell at Jesus' knees and said, "Go away from me, Lord; I am a sinful man!" ⁹ For he and all his companions were astonished at the catch of fish they had taken, ¹⁰ and so were James and John, the sons of Zebedee, Simon's partners. [185]

Upon this confession of sinfulness, this heartfelt emotional outpouring of unworthiness, Jesus provides comfort and redirection. Jesus speaks directly to Simon Peter at the beginning of His public ministry and foretells the future of the contrite man.

Then Jesus said to Simon, "Don't be afraid; from now on you will fish for people." ¹¹ So they pulled their boats up on shore, left everything and followed him. [186]

Luke provides us with an incredible perspective on the calling of Simon Peter, highlighting the moments depicted at the end of John's Gospel with renewed clarity.

Back to John

Let's fast forward about three years into the future and turn back to continue examining John 21. Remember, in this moment where we follow Peter in John's account, it is after the crucifixion, beyond the burial, and after the resurrection.

Peter, formerly known as Simon and previously a professional fisherman, goes back to his old ways. He leads about half of the other disciples.

They go fishing.

They catch nothing.

Then, mirroring the day of his initial calling from Jesus, an unknown man shouts from the shore to inquire if they have caught anything.

Frustrated, they reply, "No." They have labored all evening with no positive results.

Their empty nets, worthless efforts, become an outward symbol of their internal turmoil. It lays bare their emptiness for all to see.

John 21:6 continues the story. The yet-to-be-recognized Jesus calls out to the men and instructs them to cast their nets once more on the opposite side of the boat. Suddenly, in an event that can only be described as miraculous and which mirrors that moment of first calling, the nets are filled beyond belief. [187]

John recognizes Jesus, and Peter springs into action. Without hesitation, as John exclaims, "It is the Lord!" Peter grabs his clothes and bounds out of the boat, swimming for the shore. The other disciples follow soon after, bringing with them a net, so full of fish it had to be towed alongside the boat. [188]

When they arrive on shore, Jesus has already prepared breakfast for them. John describes the meal as consisting of fish and bread cooked over "burning coals." [189] I love how Jesus already has a meal prepared before the boat even gets there. It feels like a call back to the miracle of the five loaves and two fish, to the moment when the 5,000 were fed. [190]

There is much in this moment to take note of before continuing on into the last verses of John's Gospel. For example, back in Luke 5:10, Jesus had commanded Peter, "… from now on you will fish for people." [191]

When we connect this moment of initial calling to John's account on the other side of the resurrection, things spring to life in a new way, and we, casting our nets more deeply into the story, catch a glimpse of two powerful truths:

1. Peter abandons the fish. He leaves them on the boat with the others and swims to Jesus. It is a reversal of Peter's attempt to return to his old ways. Here, we see a man struggling with repentance for his past decisions.
2. At the same moment, Peter's abandonment of his calling to "fish for people" is brought to the surface. [192] Peter, in his night of fishing with the boys, has abandoned his Jesus-ordained calling. He has forgotten about the literal net full of fish, just as he has seemingly rejected his greater calling.

In these seemingly opposite realities, we see both the high cost of turning away from Jesus: a huge, miraculous haul of fish is being left behind; and we witness the immediately repentant Peter throwing himself headlong into the waters of repentance to swim to Jesus.

This is hope and healing for a man struggling through depression and anxiety. Peter is continuing to heal even as he fights through the consequences of his own past mistakes. The two moments seem inextricably bound to one another.

It helps us here to put ourselves in Peter's shoes. In his defense, the man had just previously denied Jesus three times. He has yet to be reinstated by Jesus; we will address that in the next chapter. Here, in this moment, Peter is back to his old ways and swimming back to shore, back to solid ground, back to the rock that is Jesus.

In choosing to return to his old habits, Peter has forgotten his calling.

In hearing the voice of Jesus, He sees again the light of hope.

In his need for transformation and despair, Peter swims back to Jesus.

He does not hesitate.

He doesn't wait for the boat.

He need not poll the audience for help.

He is propelled into action.

Meanwhile, the work on Earth continues. John points out that the other disciples are left "towing the net full of fish" to the shore. [193] If we allow the fish to continue to be metaphors for souls, we are blessed with the assurance that the work is not dependent upon one person.

To be clear, God's work on Earth is not dependent upon Peter's decision to follow or fail. Judas Iscariot's betrayal of Jesus also made that clear.

It may not be dependent upon Peter or any one person, yet the calling of Christ remains for all. He invites all of us to join in the harvest and to be a part of His Kingdom. To this point, in John 21:10, we see Jesus commanding Peter to return to his work.

> [10] Jesus said to them, "Bring some of the fish you have just caught."
> [11] So Simon Peter climbed back into the boat and dragged the net

ashore. It was full of large fish, 153, but even with so many the net was not torn. [194]

Jesus has breakfast with the men as they enjoy the harvest of God's provision for them.

Jesus, as previously mentioned, had already prepared some food. His command to Peter is, therefore, a continuation of the work. It demonstrates His divine interest in seeing Peter restored into the loving continuation of what Jesus has already started.

Following Jesus

There is much here for the follower of Christ to consider.

We see the disciples, disconnected and distraught, and they have lost their focus.

They go back to their old ways and, in those familiar habits, are found lacking.

They catch no fish.

They have no food.

They have no hope.

Then, Jesus re-enters the story. They do not decline His invitation. We need to consider and emulate this simple truth: even in their despair, the disciples obeyed Him.

As they turn from their old selves and begin to follow Him again, they experience renewal. Suddenly, they have a tremendous catch! They have physical and spiritual food; one observation would be to note the temporal and eternal sustenance of God's provision.

More deeply, they have been restored with complete hope and assurance.

Through John's thoughtful and thorough account, we see the disciples
find clarity in this moment. John makes note of this by remarking, in
John 21:12:

> "... None of the disciples dared ask him, 'Who are you?' They knew it
> was the Lord." [195]

The application here is profound, and we must consider it.

So often, we are easily distracted by the things of this world. We are hin-
dered by our earthly perspective, which limits us to seeing only what is
in front of us.

However, Jesus wants to step into each moment and call us back to
Him.

He beckons us back to His purpose, back to His light, back to His love.

Alone, we may toil and labor. We might exhaust every tool at our dis-
posal and work until we collapse under the burden of our efforts. Our
strength alone is never enough.

In our human-based efforts, we will always be left wanting more. There
is a limit to what we can do on our own.

Like the nets nearly bursting to contain all of the catch, we discover that
in Jesus, there is always more.

Jesus invites us to simply follow Him.

His call to us is the same as it always has been. It is to leave ourselves behind and to follow His perfect Way. We are to learn from Him and to

walk after Him. We are called to leave behind our desires, despairs, and disasters completely.

All four of the Gospel writers take note of Jesus' calling to follow Him. Matthew, Mark, Luke, and John bring this simple message into focus.

Christ's calling for us today continues:

> [19] "Come, follow me,"... "and I will send you out to fish for people."
> [196]

Today, every day, Jesus invites us to follow Him. It is not just for our own eventual good ends. We are to follow Him and invite others to do the same.

If you are like the fishermen Jesus calls to at the beginning of His ministry, just beginning your journey of following Jesus, He says to you, "Come follow me."

If you are like the Apostles at the end of John's powerful account of Jesus' ministry, struggling to stay the course, despairing, or maybe just distracted by the world. Even in your brokenness, Jesus says, lay down your nets, turn from your old ways, and I will remind you of a better way. He says to you, "Come follow me."

If you are like Peter, completely off course. If you have fallen back down the slippery slope of trying to build your own path forward. If you are down but longing to be restored. Well, I have very good news for you as well. Jesus calls from the shore. He says, "Drag the fish ashore." He says, "Come as you are."

"Begin again, let's start the day together."

"Together," Jesus proclaims, "Let's start over."

"Come, follow Me!"

13

This Is Love

John 21:15-25, 1 Peter 1:22-25 & 2:4-10

Enjoying breakfast at a small camp along the coast, we can only imagine what the disciples must have felt. Simultaneously, the realization that Jesus is not actually setting up a worldly kingdom, like they had expected of the promised Messiah, was suddenly coupled with the love they had experienced and witnessed.

In their brokenness, they had reverted to their old, familiar habits. The confused actions of the disciples, going fishing instead of moving forward, are a poignant reminder of the decision each of us must make when following Jesus. Do we embrace the passing of the old and allow the new to point us onward, or do we give up?

For the disciples, this moment of indecision, as captured in John's final chapter, invites us into a final lesson of God's perfect love. Jesus enters the story. He uses the moment to remind them of His calling. He has called them to be completely changed and transformed. He has sent them to become "fishers of men." [197]

Recapping the previous chapter, a man was standing on the shore. He was unrecognized. Then, this stranger called to the men in the boat, with nets empty of success and full of despair. He gives them a simple instruction; it is one they choose to obey. As they do, their nets are miraculously filled and overflowing.

John, the gospel writer, is the first to recognize Jesus.

Peter, by now known for his brashness, immediately jumps in and begins swimming to the shore.

Soon after, the others follow. They bring the boats, towing the haul of fish with them.

Breakfast is served and, importantly, Jesus restores their purpose and reminds them of their calling.

Jesus always gives His followers purpose. He gives meaning to life.

The disciples are failing and despairing. They are filled with worry and fear. So, it begs the question: how do the disciples pick themselves up and move forward?

Their ability to move forward, to embrace the all-encompassing love of God, is revealed to us as Jesus reinstates Peter.

The Rock

Peter's journey parallels Jesus' ministry from the first to the final chapter of John.

In John's opening chapter, we discover the moment of Peter's calling, and it is coupled with a moment of prophecy. When Jesus first meets Peter, He looks at him and says,

"You are Simon son of John. You will be called Cephas" (which, when translated, is Peter).[198]

"Cephas" in Aramaic was translated as "rock." Jesus is foreshadowing a later moment when Simon will be known as Peter, and Peter will make a bold proclamation.[199]

Jesus invites the man known as Simon, Cephas, Peter to follow Him, and, embracing his new identity, he follows.

While John only briefly mentions this name change for Peter in the introduction of his friend, perhaps to bring more focus onto Jesus' teachings, the other gospel writers go into much more detail. This is not perceived as a conflict in the story. The four gospels tell the story of Jesus from their unique eyewitness accounts.

In Matthew's account, for example, we read about a later moment when Jesus first publicly calls Simon by his new name: Peter. Matthew was a disciple who was added to the group later than the initial introductory moment recorded in John's gospel. In Matthew's writing, we also see an emphasis on the "why" behind the transformative name change.

Matthew 16:13-20 enlightens us to an intimate moment when Jesus was speaking directly with His disciples. He inquires of them:

13 ... "Who do people say the Son of Man is?"

14 They replied, "Some say John the Baptist; others say Elijah; and still others, Jeremiah or one of the prophets."

15 "But what about you?" he asked. "Who do you say I am?"

16 Simon Peter answered, "You are the Messiah, the Son of the living God."

[17] Jesus replied, "Blessed are you, Simon son of Jonah, for this was not revealed to you by flesh and blood, but by my Father in heaven. [18] And I tell you that you are Peter, and on this rock I will build my church, and the gates of Hades will not overcome it. [19] I will give you the keys of the kingdom of heaven; whatever you bind on earth will be bound in heaven, and whatever you loose on earth will be loosed in heaven." [20] Then he ordered his disciples not to tell anyone that he was the Messiah. [200]

Jesus is telling Peter, His disciples, and through the written Word that has been handed down over the centuries, even us, that Peter is of special significance and his confession of Jesus as "...the Messiah, the Son of the living God, " is foundational. [201]

Simon becomes Peter.

Simon, upon meeting Jesus for the first time in John's account, is foretold by Jesus to be an important leader in the foundation of the church.

This is not the only prediction Jesus made about Peter. Later in John's gospel, Jesus also predicts Peter's denial. It is also relevant to consider as we examine the final chapter of John to its completion.

In John 13:34-38, Jesus has just told His disciples that He will be going away. [202] Then, He gives them (and us) a new command.

[34] "A new command I give you: Love one another. As I have loved you, so you must love one another. [35] By this everyone will know that you are my disciples, if you love one another." [203]

Upon hearing this new commandment, Peter seems to be stuck on the fact Jesus has just told them that He is leaving. This becomes clear because, in this same moment, Peter doesn't ask Jesus to teach them about love. Peter doesn't inquire: "How do we love one another?"

No.

Quite by contrast, Peter is consumed only by the details of what he perceives as a personal loss.

> [36] Simon Peter asked him [Jesus], "Lord, where are you going?"
>
> Jesus replied, "Where I am going, you cannot follow now, but you will follow later."
>
> [37] Peter asked, "Lord, why can't I follow you now? I will lay down my life for you."
>
> [38] Then Jesus answered, "Will you really lay down your life for me? Very truly ... [204]

Before we go on, remember these "Very truly," or "Truly, truly", or "Verily verily" statements all come from the Greek "amen." They are the "so be it" at the end of a prayer. As a reminder, Jesus' saying "Amen," translated to "Very truly" in our English text, is Jesus proclaiming that what He is about to say is "A fact that is indisputable." [205]

Pausing to reflect on the gravity of what is to come is essential. Jesus' words to Peter continue:

> [38] Very truly I tell you, before the rooster crows, you will disown me three times! [206]

Jesus is predicting Peter's future failure. It has the weight of prophecy from One who sees and knows what is to come.

Later, in John 18, we read about the moment when Peter denied Jesus. On the night of His failed confession, the rooster does in fact crow. The final third crow brings with it, like the sun at dawn, the memory of this moment. It sheds light on both the power of Jesus' words and the true character of Peter.

Peter, Cephas, the one to whom Jesus said in Matthew's account:

> "... on this rock I will build my church, and the gates of Hades will not overcome it." [207]

In John 18, this same rock of a man stumbles. The bold Peter fails. He denies Jesus, just as foretold.

The rock is broken.

Love Rises

Considering the backstory of Peter sheds much light on understanding the final verses of the last chapter of John. In fact, they reveal to us the true meaning of love.

For necessary emphasis, let's consider what we know about Peter.

Peter is called to serve and follows Jesus.

Peter is lifted high as an example to the other disciples.

Peter is also predicted to fail.

Peter then, in a moment that crushes him, crashes and burns.

That is Peter's backstory. It undoubtedly frames the final text of John 21.

Here, within the Gospel writer's last words, we discover it is not just "the man, Simon Peter" that Jesus intends to use to build His church. Rather, we see it is the powerful example of God's complete love, grace, and mercy poured out with absolute forgiveness. This example, made evident in the former denier of Jesus, works as an exclamation point to God's message of redemptive love.

In Jesus, complete love is shown to be a gift for even a traitorous person, someone like Peter, who had failed Christ in a time of great need.

Peter is having breakfast with Jesus. Along with him are the other disciples who had followed Peter in his night-long failed fishing excursion. John, author and eyewitness of this account, is also present.

The sun, rising in the east, brings with it light and the start of a new day.

The world is being refreshed by the dawn sun, and as the dew settles about them, the men gathered also experience a type of restoration. It is as if love itself has arisen.

They must be exhausted. They have settled down from the initial excitement of seeing Jesus and the race to the shore with nets overflowing with their catch. It had been a long night of work and no sleep with a spike of emotion. In their second wind of the early morning, they are finally able to relax.

Peter, having dove into the water to swim to Jesus urgently, is slowly drying off by the fire. This impromptu swim surely started his morning off afresh.

Together on the shore, they finish their meal. The familiar textures of their past lives surround them and envelope their senses. The sound of the water gently lapping at the shore sings to them an ancient harmony. The fresh aroma of the damp earth and the wafting smoke of the morning campfire fill their nostrils with nostalgia. The dawn sun, hue with its many colors, illuminates the day, and the many colors of nature begin to emerge from shadow.

Across the fire, sits Jesus. They look and behold the face of God resurrected in the form of a human.

He has been their teacher, their friend, their Lord, their Master.

They have followed Him, having left all other things behind. Now, in this new day, here they sit. They are in the presence of both their old lives and the familiarity of the past, and at the same time, considering the future and God in the flesh.

It is a moment unlike any other in all of human history.

This is Love

Into the perfection of this moment, Jesus speaks. He begins what, to the casual observer, may appear as an interrogation. It is, in fact, a discourse of restoration, designed to reveal the meaning of true love.

Jesus, in John 21:15, looks across the campfire and into the eyes of Simon Peter. Then, He speaks:

> ¹⁵ ... "Simon son of John, do you love me more than these?" [208]

First off, it is worth noting that Jesus is referring to Peter by Peter's original name. He is calling him "Simon son of John." This is, perhaps, to remind Peter of who he is. Rather, Jesus is reminding Peter of who he was before Jesus. Jesus doesn't call the man revisiting his past life as a fisherman: Peter. No, He gets back to the very root of the man. Reminding him of where he began.

Secondly, it is worth noting here, and highlighting the emphasis of this study on "love," that Jesus uses the Greek verb *agape*. *Agape* is a word translated into English simply as love. However, its truest meaning is of an absolute and perfect love. It is love in the utmost and even in a sacrificial sense. *Agape* is not physical, intimate love, nor passing feelings of love. It is a word used throughout the Bible to describe God's absolute and self-sacrificing love. [209]

For example, the writer of John uses *agape* in John 12:43 to explain how the Jewish leaders had rejected Jesus. John 12:43 says:

"⁴³... for they loved human praise more than praise from God." [210]

The word translated here as "loved" originates from the Greek word *agape*. It implies love in a self-sacrificing and ultimate sense. The context is that those rejecting Jesus did so because the highest form of love they had was fulfilled in the eyes of others, more than in a relationship with God.

Another, more positive example, comes from Jesus in His new command to the disciples. In John 13:34-35, Christ uses *agape* to explain how we should love one another. Jesus says:

> ³⁴"A new command I give you: Love one another. As I have loved you, so you must love one another. ³⁵ By this everyone will know that you are my disciples, if you love one another." [211]

Each translated instance of "love" in this passage originates from the Greek word: *agape*. Jesus is not telling us to love one another in the same way we love our pets or even our favorite foods. He is talking about perfect and self-sacrificing love. It is love in the ultimate and perfect sense.

Jesus, in questioning Peter, asks, "Do you *agape*-love Me?"

How does Peter respond?

John 21:15 reveals to us Peter's answer and another Greek word translated into English simply as "love."

> ... "Yes, Lord," he said, "you know that I love you." [212]

Peter's declaration, perhaps in exasperation, that Jesus "knows" is translated from the Greek verb *oida*. [213] It implies a deeper understanding. It is as if Peter is saying to Jesus, "You know, you have seen through my past actions, it has been made evident to you that I love you."

More urgently, we must take note here that Peter says *phileo*; he does not reply using the same higher level of love, *agape*. *Phileo* is also a Greek word translated into English simply as love. However, its meaning conveys a lower-level type of love. Peter saying to Jesus, "I *phileo*-love you," is confessing a type of brotherly love or deep, friendly affection that does not necessarily communicate self-sacrifice in its love. [214]

Peter, in effect, is saying, "Jesus, you have just witnessed my betrayal and obviously, you know, you witnessed, I do not sacrificially love you the way you love me; the best I can do is love you as a brother."

Peter confesses deep affection for Jesus, but at the same time, admits the limits of his love have been displayed in his past failures. Specifically, we can safely assert that the denial of Jesus on the night of His betrayal must have been in the forethought of his words.

Jesus does not skip a beat.

He responds to Peter with grace and love. He even commands Peter to "Feed [or do the most basic care of providing food for] my lambs..." [215] Incidentally, the Greek word used for lamb here simply means a little lamb. It implies innocence and a lack of power, much like a child. [216]

A second time, Jesus addresses Peter as "Simon, son of John."

A second time, Jesus asks him, "... do you *agape*-love me?"

A second time, Peter is unable to confess the same level of perfect love.

A second time, Peter matches Jesus' *agape* love with *phileo* brotherly love, pointing out again that Jesus has already witnessed the level of love the man may have aspired to reach, but ultimately failed to demonstrate.

This dialogue leaves us with a sense that Peter is attempting to friend-zone Jesus. [217]

However, a slight bit of empathy allows one to imagine the tears welling up in Peter's eyes as, once more, he confesses the limitations of his love. He says again:

"Yes, Lord, you know that I love you." [218]

This second time, however, Jesus changes his response to Peter. He tells the man to

... "Take care of my sheep." [219]

The meaning here, in a command such as "take care," implies shepherding or tending. Figuratively, it is to lead, guide, or even rule. Additionally, Jesus changes from telling Peter to mind the little baby lambs to include the entire flock of sheep. [220] He broadens the grace and calling, even while Peter is struggling to recover, even as Peter continues to confess his limitations of reciprocal love.

A third time, Jesus asks Peter, "... do you love me?" [221]

Here, however, a remarkable change occurs. It is easy to miss in the English translation.

The third time, when Jesus inquires of Peter whether He is loved, Jesus changes from using the Greek word *agape*. Here, Jesus meets Peter where he is and asks Peter, "Do you *phileo*-love me?" "Do you love me with brotherly affection?"

This is love demonstrated for all who will consider it. Jesus loves us without flaw. Yet, even in our brokenness, when we can not reciprocate that perfect love, He meets us where we are and extends to us an invitation.

While we might miss this seemingly subtle change of phrase due to an unfortunate limitation in the English language, it is clear Peter feels the weight of it. John tells us that Jesus' third inquiry, and the change in tone implied from *agape* to *phileo*, has the effect of hurting Peter.

Peter again replies to Jesus and says, "You know..." Of course, the Greek language also highlights the full meaning of this statement. Peter says to Jesus, "Lord, you know all things... " and uses *ginosko*, a verb used to imply full and all-encompassing knowledge on a matter. [222]

The expansion of the dialogue in John 21:17 might read more like this:

> ... "Lord, you know [completely understand] all things; you know [again, *oida*, the earlier mentioned Greek word, is used here. It implies you have seen through my past actions, and you have experienced] ... that I love you. [Once more using *phileo* love]. [223]

If you allow me to simplify it further, to gain a more complete understanding, we can grasp this broader context. Peter says to Jesus:

> ... "Lord, you know and completely understand all things; you have seen and witnessed from my past actions, that I am only capable of a *phileo*-love for you; I love you dearly, but was not able to sacrifice myself in my love for You." [224]

To this, Jesus responds affirmatively again and points the man forward.

> Jesus said, "Feed my sheep." [225]

This time, as Jesus points Peter forward, Jesus again refers to the entire flock of sheep, meaning all who may follow the shepherd.

By the third interrogatory, bearing repetition by both parties, Peter has humbly admitted the limits of his imperfect, human love. He acknowledges he was not able to die for Jesus, like he originally said he would do. Yet, and we dare not miss this, in his weakness, Peter still loves Jesus as intimately as possible.

Peter, and by extension all readers of John's gospel, have also become aware of a profound truth. In Jesus Christ, there are no limitations to love. Even our failures have no bearing on the grace available in Jesus Christ.

This is love, we are reminded, and it is complete and full of grace.

The weight of this love is brought home to us as we read another "very truly" statement of absolute fact. It is when Jesus fully reinstates Peter:

> [18] Very truly I tell you, when you were younger you dressed yourself and went where you wanted; but when you are old you will stretch out your hands, and someone else will dress you and lead you where you do not want to go." [19] Jesus said this to indicate the kind of death by which Peter would glorify God. Then he said to him, "Follow me!"
> [226]

Finally, Jesus brings us full circle.

Having met Peter where he was, both literally and spiritually, Jesus invites the man to advance. He said to him, and one can imagine the way these words must have landed anew on the restored Peter. Jesus, looking at Peter with complete and forgiving love, uses the very words He spoke to Peter at the beginning of their relationship.

> ... "Follow me!" [227]

God Called Love

This brings us to the end of John's eyewitness account of Jesus Christ.

In a later letter, attributed by most to the same author as the Gospel of John, we read even more about God's love.

1 John brings to light the nature of God's perfect love.

It helps us to answer a final set of questions:

- How can we apply Jesus' message of love to our lives today?
- How does it change every day we are given?

In 1 John, the author states no less than two times that "God is love." [228]

This love is made evident in the lives of those who follow Him, not in our fear of punishment, nor of death, nor of anything. Love is evident in our love for one another. [229]

At my small church, situated on a gentle, rolling hill in southern Indiana, I shared this message of love. Together, we have tested it out. We have sought to live this message of love amongst one another.

We have succeeded, albeit imperfectly.

On Good Friday, a year or two ago, those of us who were gathered for worship had a moment of confession. We wrote our mistakes, what we considered the guilty verdict over our lives, onto pieces of paper. Then, somewhat dramatically and in a moment wrecked with emotion, we took those slips of paper to a cross made of two cedar posts. As we continued in worship, we nailed our sins to that old, rugged cross with the most menacing-looking instruments we could find.

To say it left an impression would be an understatement. Many of us were in tears.

A few days later, on Easter Sunday, we revisited that moment during a time of communion. The cross was still on display. Those cards were still nailed up, as a gruesome reminder of the need to celebrate Resurrection Sunday.

In preparation for our moment of remembrance, I tore those cards off the nails and threw them at the foot of the cross. My intent was to help us all see how the message of Jesus, the blood of Jesus, washes away our sins.

In Jesus' perfect love, our past mistakes are no longer a concern. They are gone. We are completely forgiven.

This profound message is evident in the story of Peter.

It is what is proclaimed by Paul.

The entire narrative of the Bible paints it clearly for all to see.

We call it "the gospel truth" or refer to it as the "good news."

Plainly put, we each are completely forgiven. God's perfect love in action is redemptive. This is the truth of Jesus Christ.

This is love.

John urges us to come and see that God is love.

Our God, a God called love, removes every past mistake.

In Him, we are forgiven.

Forgiven of pride.

Forgiven of envy.

Forgiven of gossip.

Forgiven of lies.

Forgiven of anger.

Forgiven of murder.

Forgiven of lust.

Forgiven of judging.

We are forgiven.

We are reborn.

We are loved.

The powerful message of Jesus Christ, brought before us in the words of the Bible, proclaims His perfect love. The end result of trying to understand the perfect love of God is overwhelming.

It is, perhaps like the nail-scarred body of our Savior, both a reminder of the past and an invitation to move forward. In Jesus, we are reminded that even the deepest scars are eternally forgiven.

They are no more.

They are washed away.

They are destroyed by God's perfect light, His life, His love.

We are, therefore, left with this incredibly powerful calling to take what we know, what we have experienced, and what we have seen... we are to take it and share the complete, sacrificial, and self-denying love of Jesus Christ with others.

Peter later writes his own letters. They provide us with a depth of insight into his changed life following that encounter on the beach with Jesus. Peter, like John, urges us to "love one another." [230]

He also writes these words from 1 Peter 2:4 and following:

⁴ As you come to him, the living Stone—rejected by humans but chosen by God and precious to him—⁵ you also, like living stones, are being built into a spiritual house to be a holy priesthood, offering spiritual sacrifices acceptable to God through Jesus Christ.

....

⁹ But you are a chosen people, a royal priesthood, a holy nation, God's special possession, that you may declare the praises of him who called you out of darkness into his wonderful light. ¹⁰ Once you were not a people, but now you are the people of God; once you had not received mercy, but now you have received mercy. [231]

This mercy and this calling, to become sanctified with holy purpose, is in fact the very reason why Jesus commanded us, in Matthew 28, to tell others about living in His radical way of *agape*, self-sacrificing love!

Matthew 28:18-20:

¹⁸ Then Jesus came to them and said, "All authority in heaven and on earth has been given to me. ¹⁹ Therefore go and make disciples of all nations, baptizing them in the name of the Father and of the Son and of the Holy Spirit, ²⁰ and teaching them to obey everything I have commanded you. And surely I am with you always, to the very end of the age." [232]

Jesus proclaims, He is with us.

Therefore, our questions from earlier become clearer:

How can we apply Jesus' message of love to our lives today?

　　We live it out with one another.

How does it change every day we are given?

It frees us from the self-centered anxiety and despair that is an affliction of our time.

These two questions, more complicated than I am letting on here, beg an additional question: Who will you tell?

If you believe Jesus is with us.

If you confess that God is love.

You must surely know that God called us to be love in action.

When we take up His calling, His purpose, His death as our life, we too become love. We take the name of Jesus Christ as our Savior for all time, and we too take on a living representation of His love.

We are invited to be love in action.

Who, then, will you tell of this great God, worthy alone to be called love?

Sources

References

Alexander, T. D. (1994). Exodus. In D. A. Carson, R. T. France, J. A. Motyer, & G. J. Wenham (Eds.), *New Bible commentary: 21st century edition*. Leicester, England; Downers Grove, IL: Inter-Varsity Press.

Blum, E. A. (1985). John. In J. F. Walvoord & R. B. Zuck (Eds.), *The Bible Knowledge Commentary: An Exposition of the Scriptures*. Wheaton, IL: Victor Books.

Blum, Edwin A. "John," in *The Bible Knowledge Commentary: An Exposition of the Scriptures*, ed. J. F. Walvoord and R. B. Zuck, vol. 2 (Wheaton, IL: Victor Books, 1985).

Burge, G. M. (1995). John. In *Evangelical Commentary on the Bible*. Grand Rapids, MI: Baker Book House.

Byrley, C. (2014). Sickness and Disability. D. Mangum, D. R. Brown, R. Klippenstein, & R. Hurst (Eds.), *Lexham Theological Wordbook*. Bellingham, WA: Lexham Press.

Cherry, Kendra, Mse. (2025, January 30). *The most common phobias from A to Z*. Verywell Mind. https://www.verywellmind.com/list-of-phobias-2795453

Friendzone | definition in the Cambridge english dictionary. (n.d.-a). https://dictionary.cambridge.org/us/dictionary/english/friendzone

Grudem, ,Wayne A., *Systematic Theology: An Introduction to Biblical Doctrine* (Leicester, England; Grand Rapids, MI: Inter-Varsity Press; Zondervan Pub. House, 2004)..

Guthrie, Donald. "John," in *New Bible Commentary: 21st Century Edition*, ed. D. A. Carson et al., 4th ed. (Leicester, England; Downers Grove, IL: Inter-Varsity Press, 1994).

Lanier, Gregory R., "Glory," in *Lexham Theological Wordbook*, ed. Douglas Mangum et al., Lexham Bible Reference Series (Bellingham, WA: Lexham Press, 2014).

Lookadoo, J. (2014). Body. D. Mangum, D. R. Brown, R. Klippenstein, & R. Hurst (Eds.), *Lexham Theological Wordbook*. Bellingham, WA: Lexham Press.

Lookadoo, J. (2014). Celestial Bodies. D. Mangum, D. R. Brown, R. Klippenstein, & R. Hurst (Eds.), *Lexham Theological Wordbook*. Bellingham, WA: Lexham Press.

Lo, Jonathan., "Deity," ed. Douglas Mangum et al., *Lexham Theological Wordbook*, Lexham Bible Reference Series (Bellingham, WA: Lexham Press, 2014).

Lycans, Zachary. "God's Metaphorical Names," in *Lexham Survey of Theology*, ed. Mark Ward et al. (Bellingham, WA: Lexham Press, 2018).

Knisley, K. (2020, February 28). *What does it mean to have a sunny side up baby?*. Healthline. https://www.healthline.com/health/pregnancy/sunny-side-up-baby

Mayo Foundation for Medical Education and Research. (2018, May 4). *Anxiety disorders*. Mayo Clinic. https://www.mayoclinic.org/diseases-conditions/anxiety/symptoms-causes/syc-20350961

Mills, D. (2014). Light and Darkness. D. Mangum, D. R. Brown, R. Klippenstein, & R. Hurst (Eds.), *Lexham Theological Wordbook*. Bellingham, WA: Lexham Press.

Oxford languages and google - english. Oxford Languages. (n.d.). https://languages.oup.com/google-dictionary-en/

Podophobia (fear of feet): Causes & symptoms. Cleveland Clinic. (2025, April 4). https://my.clevelandclinic.org/health/diseases/22707-podophobia-fear-of-feet

Strong, J. (2009). *A Concise Dictionary of the Words in the Greek Testament and The Hebrew Bible*. Bellingham, WA: Logos Bible Software.

Souter, A. (1917). *A Pocket Lexicon to the Greek New Testament*. Oxford: Clarendon Press.

The Holy Bible: English Standard Version. (2016). Wheaton, IL: Crossway Bibles.

The New International Version. (2011). Grand Rapids, MI: Zondervan.

WebMD. (n.d.). *Anxiety causes and prevention*. WebMD. https://www.webmd.com/anxiety-panic/guide/causes-anxiety

80+ gen z slang words and how to use them. 80+ Gen Z Slang words, lingo and phrases and how to use them. (n.d.). https://www.kittl.com/article/80-gen-z-slang-words-and-how-to-use-them

Endnotes

1. Burge, G. M. (1995). John. In *Evangelical Commentary on the Bible* (Vol. 3, pp. 841–842). Grand Rapids, MI: Baker Book House. ↑

2. *The New International Version* (Grand Rapids, MI: Zondervan, 2011), Mk 1:19–20. ↑

3. Blum, E. A. (1985). John. In J. F. Walvoord & R. B. Zuck (Eds.), *The Bible Knowledge Commentary: An Exposition of the Scriptures* (Vol. 2, p. 271). Wheaton, IL: Victor Books. ↑

4. *The New International Version*. (2011). (Jn 20:30–31). Grand Rapids, MI: Zondervan. ↑

5. Ibid. Jn 15:26–27. ↑

6. Ibid. 1 Jn 4:7–8. ↑

7. Ibid. 1 Jn 4:8-12. ↑

8. Ibid. 1 Jn 4:12. ↑

9. Ibid. 1 Jn 4:15–21. ↑

10. Ibid. 1 Jn 4:16–18. ↑

11. Logos - *3056.* λόγος **lŏgŏs**, *log´-os*; from *3004*; something *said* (including the *thought*); by impl. a *topic* (subject of discourse), also *reasoning* (the mental faculty) or *motive*; by extens. a *computation*; spec. (with the art. in John) the Divine *Expression* (i.e. *Christ*):—account, cause, communication, × concerning, doctrine, fame, × have to do, intent, matter, mouth, preaching, question, reason, \+ reckon, remove, say (-ing), shew, × speaker, speech, talk, thing, + none of these things move me, tidings, treatise, utterance, word, work.

    Source: Strong, J. (2009). *A Concise Dictionary of the Words in the Greek Testament and The Hebrew Bible* (Vol. 1, p. 45). Bellingham, WA: Logos Bible Software. ↑

12. Ibid. ↑

13. Phos - φῶς (*phōs*). n. neut. **light.** *Agent which shines and makes visibility possible.*

    Light is the brightness which enables human beings to see (Eph 5:13). The nt metaphorically describes Jesus as light (*phōs*; e.g., Luke 2:32; John 8:12; Eph 5:13–14); light (*phōs*) is also used as a metaphor for order and truth.

    Source: Lookadoo, J. (2014). Celestial Bodies. D. Mangum, D. R. Brown, R. Klippenstein, & R. Hurst (Eds.), *Lexham Theological Wordbook*. Bellingham, WA: Lexham Press. ↑

14. Skotia - σκοτία (*skotia*). n. fem. **darkness.** *Refers to the state characterized by the partial or complete absence of light.*

    The term is used twice in the nt in the ordinary sense of physical darkness (John 6:17; 20:1). *Skotia* is also used to describe secrecy or privacy (Matt 10:27;

Luke 12:3), the state of spiritual and moral ignorance (John 8:12; 12:35) and the sphere of moral and spiritual darkness that represents the state of the world apart from Christ (1 John 1:5; 2:8, 9, 11).

Source: Mills, D. (2014). Light and Darkness. D. Mangum, D. R. Brown, R. Klippenstein, & R. Hurst (Eds.), *Lexham Theological Wordbook*. Bellingham, WA: Lexham Press. ↑

15. *The New International Version.* (2011). (Jn 1:1–18). Grand Rapids, MI: Zondervan. ↑

16. Ibid. Jn 1:1–18. ↑

17. Kolpos - *2859.* κόλπος **kŏlpŏs**, *kol'-pos*; appar. a prim. word; the *bosom*; by anal. a *bay*:—bosom, creek.

Source: Strong, J. (2009). *A Concise Dictionary of the Words in the Greek Testament and The Hebrew Bible* (Vol. 1, p. 43). Bellingham, WA: Logos Bible Software. ↑

18. *The New International Version* (Grand Rapids, MI: Zondervan, 2011), Jn 1:23. ↑

19. Ibid. Is 40:1–5. ↑

20. Ibid. Jn 1:26-27. ↑

21. Ibid. Jn 1:29-34. ↑

22. Erchomai - *2064.* ἔρχομαι **ĕrchŏmai**, *er'-khom-ahee*; mid. of a prin. verb (used only in the pres. and imperf. tenses, the others being supplied by a kindred [mid.]

ἐλεύθομαι **ĕlĕuthŏmai**, *el-yoo'-thom-ahee*; or [act.]

Eltho - ἔλθω **ĕlthō**, *el'-tho*; which do not otherwise occur); to *come* or *go* (in a great variety of applications, lit. and fig.):—accompany, appear, bring, come, enter, fall out, go, grow, × light, × next, pass, resort, be set.

Source: James Strong, *A Concise Dictionary of the Words in the Greek Testament and The Hebrew Bible* (Bellingham, WA: Logos Bible Software, 2009), 32. ↑

23. Souter, A. (1917). *A Pocket Lexicon to the Greek New Testament* (p. 97). Oxford: Clarendon Press. ↑

24. *The New International Version.* (2011). (Jn 1:29–31). Grand Rapids, MI: Zondervan. ↑

25. Ibid. Jn 1:19–51. ↑

26. Ibid. Jn 2:14. ↑

27. Ibid. Ge 1:26–27. ↑

28. This text was adapted from *The New International Version.* (2011). (Jn 2:13-25) by Michael J. Chanley. ↑

29. *The New International Version.* (2011). (Jn 1:1–5). Grand Rapids, MI: Zondervan. ↑

30. Ibid. Jn 3:2. ↑

31. Ibid. Jn 3:3-4. ↑

32. Ibid. Jn 3:5-7. ↑

33. Ibid. Jn 3:8. ↑

34. Please see Numbers 21:4-9 for further context if you are unfamiliar with this story. ↑

35. *The New International Version.* (2011). (Jn 3:16). Grand Rapids, MI: Zondervan. ↑

36. Ibid. Jn 3:17. ↑

37. Pas - *3956.* πᾶς **pas**, *pas*; includ. all the forms of declension; appar. a prim. word; *all, any, every,* the *whole*:—all (manner of, means), alway (-s), any (one), × daily, + ever, every (one, way), as many as, + no (-thing), × throughly, whatsoever, whole, whosoever.

    Source: James Strong, *A Concise Dictionary of the Words in the Greek Testament and The Hebrew Bible* (Bellingham, WA: Logos Bible Software, 2009), 56. ↑

38. *The New International Version.* (2011). (Jn 3:1–21). Grand Rapids, MI: Zondervan. ↑

39. Ibid. Jn 3:27–36. Emphasis added by the author. ↑

40. *The New International Version.* (2011). (Jn 3:3). Grand Rapids, MI: Zondervan. ↑

41. Ibid. Jn 3:5–6. ↑

42. Amen - *281.* ἀμήν **amēn**, *am-ane'*; of Heb. or. [543]; prop. *firm,* i.e. (fig.) *trustworthy*; adv. *surely* (often as interj. *so be it*):—amen, verily.

    Source: James Strong, *A Concise Dictionary of the Words in the Greek Testament and The Hebrew Bible* (Bellingham, WA: Logos Bible Software, 2009), 10. ↑

43. *The New International Version.* (2011). (Jn 3:3 & 5–6). Grand Rapids, MI: Zondervan. ↑

44. *The Holy Bible: English Standard Version.* (2016). (Ps 32:1–5). Wheaton, IL: Crossway Bibles. ↑

45. *The New International Version.* (2011). (Jn 21:25). Grand Rapids, MI: Zondervan. ↑

46. Ibid. Jn 4:4–7. ↑

47. Ibid. Jn 4:13–14. ↑

48. Ibid. Jn 4:46–47. ↑

49. Ibid. Jn 4:50. ↑

50. Ibid. Jn 5:3–9. ↑

51. Astheneia - ἀσθένεια (*astheneia*). n. fem. **sickness, weakness.** *Refers to a weakness or disability, often due to natural limitations or illness.*

Source: Byrley, C. (2014). Sickness and Disability. D. Mangum, D. R. Brown, R. Klippenstein, & R. Hurst (Eds.), *Lexham Theological Wordbook*. Bellingham, WA: Lexham Press. ↑

52.   Ibid. ↑

53.   *The New International Version*. (2011). (Jn 5:3–9). Grand Rapids, MI: Zondervan. ↑

54.   Amen - *281.* ἀμήν **amēn**, *am-ane'*; of Heb. or. [543]; prop. *firm*, i.e. (fig.) *trustworthy*; adv. *surely* (often as interj. *so be it*):—amen, verily.

    Source: James Strong, *A Concise Dictionary of the Words in the Greek Testament and The Hebrew Bible* (Bellingham, WA: Logos Bible Software, 2009), 10. ↑

55.   *The New International Version*. (2011). (Jn 5:19-23). Grand Rapids, MI: Zondervan. ↑

56.   Ibid. Jn 5:24. ↑

57.   Ibid. Jn 5:25-27. ↑

58.   See Exodus 16 for reference. ↑

59.   See Exodus 14 for reference. ↑

60.   Amen - *281.* ἀμήν **amēn**, *am-ane'*; of Heb. or. [543]; prop. *firm*, i.e. (fig.) *trustworthy*; adv. *surely* (often as interj. *so be it*):—amen, verily.

    Source: James Strong, *A Concise Dictionary of the Words in the Greek Testament and The Hebrew Bible* (Bellingham, WA: Logos Bible Software, 2009), 10. ↑

61.   *The New International Version*. (2011). (Jn 6:26-27). Grand Rapids, MI: Zondervan. ↑

62.   Ibid. Jn 6:32-33. ↑

63.   Ibid. Jn 6:35. ↑

64.   Ibid. Jn 6:47-51. ↑

65.   Ibid. Jn 6:53-58. ↑

66.   Ibid. Jn 6:68-69. ↑

67.   Ibid. Ex 3:2b–6. ↑

68.   Ibid. Ex 3:11. ↑

69.   Ibid. Ex 3:11–12. ↑

70.   Ibid. Ex 3:13-15. ↑

71.   Yahweh - יהוה (*yhwh*). n. masc. **Yahweh.** *The proper name of Israel's deity.* God revealed this name for himself when he appeared to Moses in the burning bush (Exod 3). It is the proper name by which Israel addressed God.

    Source: Jonathan Lo, "Deity," ed. Douglas Mangum et al., *Lexham Theological Wordbook*, Lexham Bible Reference Series (Bellingham, WA: Lexham Press, 2014). ↑

72.   *The New International Version* (Grand Rapids, MI: Zondervan, 2011), Ex 3:14. ↑

73. Ibid. Ex 3:13–15. ↑

74. Ibid. Ex 3:14. ↑

75. Alexander, T. D. (1994). Exodus. In D. A. Carson, R. T. France, J. A. Motyer, & G. J. Wenham (Eds.), *New Bible commentary: 21st century edition* (4th ed., p. 97). Leicester, England; Downers Grove, IL: Inter-Varsity Press. ↑

76. Ibid. ↑

77. Zachary Lycans, "God's Metaphorical Names," in *Lexham Survey of Theology*, ed. Mark Ward et al. (Bellingham, WA: Lexham Press, 2018). ↑

78. Ibid. ↑

79. Alexander, T. D. (1994). Exodus. In D. A. Carson, R. T. France, J. A. Motyer, & G. J. Wenham (Eds.), *New Bible commentary: 21st century edition* (4th ed., p. 97). Leicester, England; Downers Grove, IL: Inter-Varsity Press. ↑

80. Ibid. ↑

81. *The New International Version.* (2011). (Jn 8:58). Grand Rapids, MI: Zondervan. ↑

82. Ibid. ↑

83. *The New International Version.* (2011). (Jn 4:25–26). Grand Rapids, MI: Zondervan. ↑

84. Ibid. Jn 6:47–48. ↑

85. Ibid. Jn 8:18. ↑

86. Ibid. Jn 8:23–24. ↑

87. Ibid. Jn 8:12b. ↑

88. See Genesis chapters 1-2 for reference. ↑

89. *The New International Version* (Grand Rapids, MI: Zondervan, 2011), Jn 1:1–5. Additional emphasis added by the author. ↑

90. *The New International Version* (Grand Rapids, MI: Zondervan, 2011), Jn 3:16–21. ↑

91. Ibid. Jn 9:1–5. ↑

92. Ibid. Jn 9:5. ↑

93. Ibid. Jn 9:8–9. ↑

94. Ibid. Jn 9:25. ↑

95. Ibid. ↑

96. *The New International Version.* (2011). (Jn 1:4). Grand Rapids, MI: Zondervan. ↑

97. *The New International Version.* (2011). (Jn 1:4-5). Grand Rapids, MI: Zondervan. Bold emphasis added by the author. ↑

98. Ibid. Jn 1:7. ↑

99. Ibid. Jn 1:8. ↑

100. *The New International Version.* (2011). (Jn 1:9-13). Grand Rapids, MI: Zondervan. Bold emphasis added by author. ↑

101. *The New International Version.* (2011). (Jn 1:12). Grand Rapids, MI: Zondervan. ↑

102. *The New International Version.* (2011). (Jn 1:4–14). Grand Rapids, MI: Zondervan. Bold emphasis added by author. ↑

103. σάρξ (*sarx*). n. fem. **flesh.** *Refers to the physical material out of which the body is composed.*
Source: Lookadoo, J. (2014). Body. D. Mangum, D. R. Brown, R. Klippenstein, & R. Hurst (Eds.), *Lexham Theological Wordbook.* Bellingham, WA: Lexham Press. ↑

104. *The New International Version.* (2011). (Jn 8:58). Grand Rapids, MI: Zondervan. ↑

105. Ibid. Jn 10:7–18. ↑

106. Ibid. ↑

107. Strong, J. (2009). *A Concise Dictionary of the Words in the Greek Testament and The Hebrew Bible* (Vol. 1, p. 35). Bellingham, WA: Logos Bible Software. ↑

108. Souter, A. (1917). *A Pocket Lexicon to the Greek New Testament* (p. 105). Oxford: Clarendon Press. ↑

109. *The New International Version.* (2011). (Jn 10:7–18). Grand Rapids, MI: Zondervan. ↑

110. Ibid. Jn 11:9–15. ↑

111. Ibid. ↑

112. Ibid. ↑

113. Ibid. ↑

114. *The New International Version.* (2011). (Jn 11:17–27). Grand Rapids, MI: Zondervan. ↑

115. Ibid. ↑

116. Ibid. ↑

117. Ibid. ↑

118. Ibid. ↑

119. Ibid. ↑

120. *The New International Version.* (2011). (Jn 12:44–50). Grand Rapids, MI: Zondervan. ↑

121. *Oxford languages and google - english.* Oxford Languages. (n.d.). https://languages.oup.com/google-dictionary-en/ ↑

122. Mayo Foundation for Medical Education and Research. (2018, May 4). *Anxiety disorders.* Mayo Clinic. https://www.mayoclinic.org/diseases-conditions/anxiety/symptoms-causes/syc-20350961 ↑

123. Ibid. ↑

124. WebMD. (n.d.). *Anxiety causes and prevention.* WebMD. https://www.webmd.com/anxiety-panic/guide/causes-anxiety ↑

125. If you need help translating some of this Gen Z and Gen Alpha slang, I suggest you do a google search or refer to this reference: https://www.kittl.com/article/80-gen-z-slang-words-and-how-to-use-them. Alternatively, take a young person out for a coffee or lunch and share this book with them. ↑

126. Kendra Cherry, Mse. (2025, January 30). *The most common phobias from A to Z*. Verywell Mind. https://www.verywellmind.com/list-of-phobias-2795453 ↑

127. *Podophobia (fear of feet): Causes & symptoms*. Cleveland Clinic. (2025, April 4). https://my.clevelandclinic.org/health/diseases/22707-podophobia-fear-of-feet ↑

128. *The New International Version*. (2011). (Jn 13:12–17). Grand Rapids, MI: Zondervan. ↑

129. For examples where the Biblical authors referred to Christianity simply as "The Way," see: Acts 9:2, 19:9 & 23, 22:4, 24:14 & 22. ↑

130. *The New International Version*. (2011). (Jn 14:1–4). Grand Rapids, MI: Zondervan. ↑

131. Ibid. Jn 14:6–7. ↑

132. Author's note: I'm paraphrasing what Jesus actually says in John 14:15: [5] "If you love me, keep my commands." ↑

133. *The New International Version*. (2011). (Jn 14:15-17). Grand Rapids, MI: Zondervan. ↑

134. Ibid. ↑

135. *The New International Version*. (2011). (Jn 15:1–17). Grand Rapids, MI: Zondervan. ↑

136. Ibid. ↑

137. Ibid. ↑

138. Knisley, K. (2020, February 28). *What does it mean to have a sunny side up baby?*. Healthline. https://www.healthline.com/health/pregnancy/sunny-side-up-baby ↑

139. For reference, see Zechariah 9:9. ↑

140. For reference to this event, see: John 12:12-15, Matthew 21:4-9, Mark 11:7-10, and Luke 19:35-38. ↑

141. *The New International Version* (Grand Rapids, MI: Zondervan, 2011), Jn 1:23. ↑

142. Ibid. Jn 1:14. ↑

143. Ibid. Jn 12:12–15. ↑

144. Ibid. Jn 12:16. ↑

145. ὡσαννά **hōsanna**, *ho-san-nah'*; of Heb. or. [3467 and 4994]; *oh save!*; *hosanna* (i.e. *hoshia-na*), an exclamation of adoration:—hosanna.
     Source: Strong, J. (2009). *A Concise Dictionary of the Words in the Greek Testament and The Hebrew Bible* (Vol. 1, p. 79). Bellingham, WA: Logos Bible Software. ↑

146.   *The New International Version.* (2011). (Jn 16:13). Grand Rapids, MI: Zondervan. ↑

147.   Ibid. Re 22:12–15. ↑

148.   Ibid. Jn 16:33. ↑

149.   For reference, The Lord's Model Prayer (Jesus teaching us how to pray) appears in Matthew 6:9-14 and Luke 11:2-4. ↑

150.   *The New International Version* (Grand Rapids, MI: Zondervan, 2011), Jn 16:33. ↑

151.   Ibid. Jn 17:1-5. ↑

152.   Ibid. Jn 17:3. ↑

153.   Gregory R. Lanier, "Glory," in *Lexham Theological Wordbook*, ed. Douglas Mangum et al., Lexham Bible Reference Series (Bellingham, WA: Lexham Press, 2014). ↑

154.   *The New International Version* (Grand Rapids, MI: Zondervan, 2011), Jn 17:6-19. ↑

155.   Ibid. Jn 17:16. ↑

156.   Ibid. Jn 17:17. ↑

157.   λόγος: The Greek term for "word" by which the apostle John referred to Jesus in John 1:1. As applied to Jesus, the term implies both the Old Testament concept of the powerful, creative word of God and the Greek idea of the organizing and unifying principle of the universe. (26B.1.c)

   Source: Wayne A. Grudem, *Systematic Theology: An Introduction to Biblical Doctrine* (Leicester, England; Grand Rapids, MI: Inter-Varsity Press; Zondervan Pub. House, 2004), 1246. ↑

158.   *The New International Version.* (2011). (Jn 1:1–2). Grand Rapids, MI: Zondervan. ↑

159.   Ibid. Jn 1:14. ↑

160.   Ibid. ↑

161.   *The New International Version.* (2011). (Jn 17:17). Grand Rapids, MI: Zondervan. ↑

162.   Ibid. Jn 16:33. ↑

163.   Ibid. Jn 17:20-23. ↑

164.   Ibid. Jn 17:24-26. ↑

165.   Ibid. Jn 13:34–35. ↑

166.   Ibid. Jn 15:17. ↑

167.   See Luke 8:2 ↑

168.   *The New International Version.* (2011). (Lk 10:38–42). Grand Rapids, MI: Zondervan. ↑

169.   Ibid. Jn 20:21–23. ↑

170.   Donald Guthrie, "John," in *New Bible Commentary: 21st Century Edition*, ed. D. A. Carson et al., 4th ed. (Leicester, England; Downers Grove, IL: Inter-Varsity Press, 1994), 1063. ↑

171.   Edwin A. Blum, "John," in *The Bible Knowledge Commentary: An Exposition of the Scriptures*, ed. J. F. Walvoord and R. B. Zuck, vol. 2 (Wheaton, IL: Victor Books, 1985), 343. ↑

172.   *The New International Version* (Grand Rapids, MI: Zondervan, 2011), Jn 20:21–23. ↑

173.   Ibid. Jn 3:16. ↑

174.   Ibid. Jn 3:17. ↑

175.   Ibid. Jn 3:16–21. ↑

176.   Ibid. 1 Jn 4:15–16. ↑

177.   Ibid. ↑

178.   *The New International Version* (Grand Rapids, MI: Zondervan, 2011), Jn 21:3. ↑

179.   Ibid. Jn 21:3-5. ↑

180.   Ibid. Lk 5:1–3a. ↑

181.   Ibid. Lk 5:3. ↑

182.   Ibid. Lk 5:4-5. ↑

183.   Ibid. Lk 5:6. ↑

184.   Ibid. Lk 5:7. ↑

185.   Ibid. Lk 5:8-10a. ↑

186.   Ibid. Lk 5:10b-11. ↑

187.   Ibid. Jn 21:6. ↑

188.   Ibid. Jn 21:7-8. ↑

189.   Ibid. Jn 21:9. ↑

190.   For reference to the feeding of the 5,000, see John 6:1-14. ↑

191.   *The New International Version* (Grand Rapids, MI: Zondervan, 2011), Lk 5:10c. ↑

192.   Ibid. ↑

193.   *The New International Version* (Grand Rapids, MI: Zondervan, 2011), Jn 21:8. ↑

194.   Ibid. Jn 21:10-11. ↑

195.   Ibid. Jn 21:12b. ↑

196.   Ibid. Mt 4:19. ↑

197.   Ibid. Mt 4:19. ↑

198.   Ibid. Jn 1:42b. ↑

199.   Κηφᾶς, *Cephas* (Aram. for *rock*), the new name given to Simon, the disciple. Source: Alexander Souter, *A Pocket Lexicon to the Greek New Testament* (Oxford: Clarendon Press, 1917), 133. ↑

200. *The New International Version*. (2011). (Mt 16:13–20). Grand Rapids, MI: Zondervan. ↑

201. Ibid. Mt. 16:16. ↑

202. Ibid. Jn 13:33. ↑

203. Ibid. Jn 13:34–35. ↑

204. Ibid. Jn 13:36-38a. ↑

205. Amen - *281*. ἀμήν **amēn**, *am-ane'*; of Heb. or. [543]; prop. *firm*, i.e. (fig.) *trustworthy*; adv. *surely* (often as interj. *so be it*):—amen, verily.

   Source: James Strong, *A Concise Dictionary of the Words in the Greek Testament and The Hebrew Bible* (Bellingham, WA: Logos Bible Software, 2009), 10. ↑

206. *The New International Version* (Grand Rapids, MI: Zondervan, 2011), Jn 13:34–38. ↑

207. Ibid. Mt. 16:18-19. ↑

208. Ibid. Jn 21:15b. ↑

209. ἀγαπάω (*agapaō*). vb. **to love**. *Involves a deep level of affection and intimacy.* This verb is the usual Septuagint translation of Hebrew אָהַב (*'āhab*, "to love"). It occurs frequently in the nt, much more often than φιλέω (*phileō*, "to love"). The verb *agapaō* can describe Jesus' love for people (e.g., Mark 10:21), the Father's love for Jesus (e.g., John 3:35), human love for God (e.g., Mark 12:30) and a broader range of love between people, including love for one's neighbor and even one's enemy (e.g., Matt 5:43–46). John calls one of Jesus' disciples (traditionally identified as John himself) "the disciple whom Jesus loved"; both *agapaō* (e.g., John 13:23) and *phileō* (John 20:2) are used in this phrase, which appears to indicate a particularly close relationship between Jesus and this disciple.

   Source: Justin Langford, "Friendship," in *Lexham Theological Wordbook*, ed. Douglas Mangum et al., Lexham Bible Reference Series (Bellingham, WA: Lexham Press, 2014). ↑

210. *The New International Version*. (2011). (Jn 12:43). Grand Rapids, MI: Zondervan. ↑

211. *The New International Version* (Grand Rapids, MI: Zondervan, 2011), Jn 13:34–35. ↑

212. Ibid. Jn 21:15. ↑

213. οἶδα (*oida*). vb. **to have seen, to know**. *Refers to the past act of seeing with the present effect of knowing what was seen.* Technically a perfect tense from εἶδον (*eidon*, "see") but used as a present (see bdag, s.v. οἶδα), *oida* occurs over 300 times in the nt. To "have seen" something in the past becomes "to know" it in the present. *Oida* often connotes not only having knowledge but also being able to understand that knowledge (Luke 2:49; Acts 3:17; Rom 6:9). In the Synoptic Gospels, Jesus equates others' seeing his

Source: Jeremiah K. Garrett, "Knowledge," in *Lexham Theological Word-book*, ed. Douglas Mangum et al., Lexham Bible Reference Series (Bellingham, WA: Lexham Press, 2014). ↑

214. φιλέω (*phileō*). vb. **to love, like, or kiss**. *Describes an affection ranging from general emotion to deep love.*

While the term can convey deep affection for another person, the range of meaning is probably narrower than αγαπάω (*agapaō*, "to love"). The type of love expressed by *phileō* can be found among relatives (Matt 10:37), and friends (John 11:3); *phileō* can also describe God's love for Christ (John 5:20). This verb occurs in the final scene of John's Gospel between Jesus and Peter (John 21:15–17). While both *phileō* and *agapaō* are used in this exchange, a distinction in meaning is unlikely. The meaning "to like to do [something]" is probably intended in Matt 6:5 (the hypocrites like [*phileō*] to pray where all can see them). The word can also mean "to kiss"; in the Synoptic parallels of Judas' betrayal in the garden (Matt 26:48; Mark 14:44; Luke 22:47), the Gospel writers indicate that Judas signaled Jesus' identity to the guards by kissing (*phileō*) him.

Source: Justin Langford, "Friendship," in *Lexham Theological Wordbook*, ed. Douglas Mangum et al., Lexham Bible Reference Series (Bellingham, WA: Lexham Press, 2014). ↑

215. *The New International Version* (Grand Rapids, MI: Zondervan, 2011), Jn 21:15. ↑

216. ἀρνίον (originally, *a little lamb*, but diminutive force was lost), *a lamb*: see ἀρήν.

Souter, A. (1917). *A Pocket Lexicon to the Greek New Testament* (p. 37). Oxford: Clarendon Press. ↑

217. Friendzone is defined as the state of being friends with someone when you would prefer a romantic or sexual relationship with them:

Source: Friendzone | definition in the Cambridge english dictionary. (n.d.-a). https://dictionary.cambridge.org/us/dictionary/english/friendzone ↑

218. *The New International Version* (Grand Rapids, MI: Zondervan, 2011), Jn 21:16. ↑

219. Ibid. Jn 21:16c. ↑

220. πρόβατον (*probaton*). n. neut. **sheep**. *In classical Greek it could refer to cattle generally, but in the New Testament it always refers to sheep or a flock of sheep.*

Source: Benjamin M. Austin, "Animals," in *Lexham Theological Wordbook*, ed. Douglas Mangum et al., Lexham Bible Reference Series (Bellingham, WA: Lexham Press, 2014). ↑

221. *The New International Version* (Grand Rapids, MI: Zondervan, 2011), Jn 21:17b. ↑

222. γινώσκω (*ginōskō*). vb. **to know, understand, acknowledge**. *Refers to having knowledge or understanding regarding a subject.*

Appearing over 225 times in the nt, *ginōskō* is the verb related to γνῶσις (*gnōsis*, "knowledge"). Although used less often in the nt than οἶδα (*oida*), *ginōskō* is the basic Greek verb for knowing.

Source: Jeremiah K. Garrett, "Knowledge," in *Lexham Theological Wordbook*, ed. Douglas Mangum et al., Lexham Bible Reference Series (Bellingham, WA: Lexham Press, 2014). ↑

223. *The New International Version* (Grand Rapids, MI: Zondervan, 2011), Jn 21:17. ↑

224. Ibid. ↑

225. *The New International Version* (Grand Rapids, MI: Zondervan, 2011), Jn 21:17c. ↑

226. Ibid. Jn 21:18-19 ↑

227. Ibid. Jn 21:19b. ↑

228. Ibid. 1 Jn 4:7–21. ↑

229. Ibid. ↑

230. *The Holy Bible: English Standard Version.* (2016). (1 Pe 1:22–25). Wheaton, IL: Crossway Bibles. ↑

231. *The New International Version.* (2011). (1 Pe 2:4-5 & 9–10). Grand Rapids, MI: Zondervan. ↑

232. Ibid. Mt 28:18–20. ↑

About the Author

Michael J. Chanley is a local pastor obsessed with teaching about God's love. His recent projects have grown from his desire to more fully understand the meaning of "God is love," as written in 1 John. His dedication to sharing what He has learned led him to author an insightful and approachable commentary on the Book of John and a stand-alone journal.

Both resources are available at **michaeljchanley.com**, or wherever books are sold:

- *God Called Love: Experience Love, In An Anxious World, Needing Grace*

- *Experiencing God Called Love: 5 Week Journal on God's Love & Guidebook to the Spiritual Practices*

After honorably serving in the Marine Corps, Michael followed his calling to serve in ministry. For over 25 years, he has served in children's and family ministry. He currently serves as the Pastor at Tunnel Hill Christian Church in Southern Indiana. It is a community dedicated to meaningful growth with a vision to "grow in faith, share hope, and to love one another as followers of Jesus." His passion for people led him to pursue degrees in history and sociology. He also earned his Master's from Lincoln Christian Seminary, where he focused on ministry, spiritual formation, and leadership.

Michael has been married for over 30 years to Rose. Together, they have three wonderful children and one grandson. On their small farm, nestled in the highlands of Southern Indiana, they keep chickens, peafowl, a chocolate lab, too many cats to count, and an apiary full of honeybees.

Chanley's books frequently appear on "new release" and "best seller" lists. An award winning speaker, he is available for a limited number of speaking engagements each year. His contact information, and other titles, can be found at **michaeljchanley.com**.

Also from Michael J. Chanley

Hope & Honeybees - Lessons of Faith From a Local Beekeeper a study on the biblical theme of hope with lessons extracted from the life of honeybees.

Escape - The Traps of Christianity an exploration in the pursuit of authentic Christianity.

Chasing Whales - A Spiritual Dive with Jonah an interactive resource designed to teach Bible study methods while diving deeply into the story of Jonah.

Please visit **michaeljchanley.com** for more details and to discover other available books and resources.

Better Together!

God Called Love: Experience Love, In An Anxious World, Needing Grace is an approachable commentary on the Book of John. Focused on God's love, it challenges both the new believer and life long sojourner, to rediscover the heart of Jesus.

Experiencing God's Love: 5 Week Journal On God's Love & Spiritual Practices Guidebook builds on the theme of love and invites you into a week's long journey of spiritual growth.

Visit **michaeljchanley.com** to order your copies now and to discover other available books and resources.

www.ingramcontent.com/pod-product-compliance
Lightning Source LLC
Chambersburg PA
CBHW031512120626
46545CB00005B/1845